THE QUEEN'S FAMILY

The Royal Family has captured the affections of the British public very largely because the people of Britain see their monarch as a daughter, sister, wife, mother and grandmother, and recognise in the Royal Family a concern for those values the family as an institution has traditionally embodied.

In *The Queen's Family* Graham and Heather Fisher, who have been writing about the Royal Family for 25 years, bring to life just those qualities that made the Royal Wedding such an astounding success and the birth of Prince William a cause for national celebration.

THE QUEEN'S FAMILY

Graham and Heather Fisher

A STAR BOOK

published by
the Paperback Division of
W. H. ALLEN & Co. Ltd

A Star Book
Published in 1983
by the Paperback Division of
W.H. Allen & Co. Ltd
A Howard and Wyndham Company
44 Hill Street, London W1X 8LB

First published in Great Britain by W.H. Allen & Co. Ltd,
1982

Printed in Great Britain by
Hunt Barnard Printing, Ltd., Aylesbury, Bucks.

ISBN 0 352 31290 4

The Photographs included in this Book are reproduced
courtesy of Syndication International

For our own
family

Contents

Foreword

To most people (because they know them only as photo-graphs in newspapers or glimpse them only at a distance), the Royal Family are hardly more real than visitors from outer space; more demi-gods than flesh-and-blood human beings.

But behind the royal façade lurks a family much like any other family. Wealthy, of course, and with a lifestyle which is perhaps light years removed from ordinary life as most of us know it, but yet as capable as anyone else of feeling happiness or sadness, hope, doubt, anger, bitterness and all the other emotions to which humanity is susceptible. They laugh, cry and bleed just like the rest of us; fall in – or out of – love, marry, have babies just like everyone else. And death, in due course, takes its inevitable toll as it does of every family.

This book is the story of the Royal Family *as a family*; from the days when the Queen was the favourite grandchild of the man she called 'Grandpapa England' to her present role as a grandmother herself; a history of the 'family web of parents and children, grandparents and grandchildren, cousins, uncles and aunts' of which she spoke so movingly on her silver wedding day.

G. and H. Fisher
Keston Park
Kent

The Queen's Family

First Generation

Grandpapa England   1865–1936. Second son of King Edward VII and Queen Alexandra. Became heir to the throne when his elder brother died in 1892, married his dead brother's fiancée 1893, ascended the throne as King George V 1910. Took the name of Windsor for himself and his family during World War I.

Gan Gan   1867–1953. By turns, Princess Victoria Mary of Teck (called 'May' in the family), Princess of Wales and Queen Mary.

Second Generation

David   1894–1972. Prince of Wales, King Edward VIII, Duke of Windsor. Succeeded to the throne in 1936 and abdicated the same year to marry a twice-divorced American, Bessie Wallis Warfield (Mrs Simpson). No children.

Bertie   1895–1952. As Duke of York, married Lady Elizabeth Bowes-Lyon (Queen Elizabeth, the Queen Mother) in 1923. Became King George VI when his brother David abdicated.

Mary   1897–1965. The Princess Royal. Married Henry, Viscount ('Lucky') Lascelles, later 6th Earl of Harewood, 1922.

Harry   1900–1974. Prince Henry, Duke of Gloucester. Married Lady Alice

10

	Montagu-Douglas-Scott (Princess Alice, Duchess of Gloucester) 1935.
George	1902–1942. Duke of Kent. Married Princess Marina of Greece 1934. Died in a World War II air crash.
John	1905–1919. Died of epilepsy while still in his teens.

Third Generation
Bertie's children:

Lilibet	Born 1926. By turns, Princess Elizabeth, Duchess of Edinburgh and Queen Elizabeth II. Married Philip, Duke of Edinburgh (formerly Philip Mountbatten and Prince Philip of Greece) 1947. Succeeded to the throne 1952 on the death of her father.
Margaret (Margo)	Born 1930. Princess Margaret Rose, Countess of Snowdon. Married photographer Antony Armstrong-Jones (later Earl of Snowdon) 1960. Divorced 1978.

Harry's children:

William	1941–1972. Prince William of Gloucester. Died in an air crash. Unmarried.
Richard	Born 1944. Prince Richard of Gloucester. Married Birgitte van Deurs (Danish) 1972. Became Duke of Gloucester on the death of his father.

George's children:

Eddy	Born 1935. Prince Edward of Kent. Became Duke of Kent on the death of his father. Married Katherine Worsley 1961.
Alex	Born 1936. Princess Alexandra of Kent. Married the Hon. Angus Ogilvy 1963.
Michael	Born 1942. Prince Michael of Kent. Married Baroness Marie-Christine von Reibnitz 1978 following the annulment of her previous marriage.

Mary's children:

George	Born 1923. Viscount Lascelles. Became Earl of Harewood on the death of his father.

| | Married Marion Stein 1949. Divorced 1967. Subsequently married Patricia Tuckwell, a divorced Australian. |
| Gerald | Born 1924. The Hon. Gerald Lascelles. Married Angela Dowding 1952. Divorced 1978. Subsequently married Mrs Elizabeth Colvin. |

Fourth Generation

The Queen's children:

Charles	Born 1948. Prince of Wales and Duke of Cornwall. Married Lady Diana Spencer 1981.
Anne	Born 1950. Princess Anne. Married Captain Mark Phillips 1973.
Andrew	Born 1960. Prince Andrew.
Edward	Born 1964. Prince Edward.

Princess Margaret's children:

| David | Born 1961. Viscount Linley. |
| Sarah | Born 1964. Lady Sarah Armstrong-Jones. |

Duke of Gloucester's children:

Alexander	Born 1974. Earl of Ulster.
Davina	Born 1977. Lady Davina Windsor.
Rose	Born 1980. Lady Rose Windsor.

Duke of Kent's children:

George	Born 1962. Earl of St Andrews.
Helen	Born 1964. Lady Helen Windsor.
Nicholas	Born 1970. Lord Nicholas Windsor.

Princess Alexandra's children:

| James | Born 1964. James Ogilvy. |
| Marina | Born 1966. Marina Ogilvy. |

Prince Michael's children:

| Frederick | Born 1979. Lord Frederick Windsor. |
| Ella | Born 1981. Lady Gabriela Windsor. |

Earl of Harewood's children:

David	Born 1950. Viscount Lascelles.
James	Born 1953. The Hon. James Lascelles. Married Fredericka Duhrrson 1973.
Robert	Born 1955. The Hon. Robert Lascelles.

Mark	Born (by second wife) 1964. The Hon. Mark Lascelles.

Gerald Lascelles:
Henry	Born 1953.

Fifth Generation
Prince Charles's son:
William	Born 1982. Prince William of Wales.

Princess Anne's children:
Peter	Born 1977. Peter Phillips.
Zara	Born 1981. Zara Phillips.

1

Grandpapa England

A small fair-haired girl stood at an upstairs window of a tall narrow Victorian house in Piccadilly, looking out at the world through a pair of binoculars almost too large for her child's hands. Through the binoculars she could see over the bushy tops of the trees in Green Park to a wing of Buckingham Palace. Her face broke into a smile as the bearded figure of a man came into view at one of the palace windows, looking back at her through another pair of binoculars.

It was the early 1930s . . . a half-century or more ago, a world war ago, a different world. Cigarettes were ten for sixpence (2.5 pence in today's decimalised coinage) and a small family car could be bought for little over £100. It was the era of Crosby's crooning, the dancing of Astaire and Rogers, with Fred Perry dominant at Wimbledon. The impact of the 'talkies' had peppered the English language with slick Americanisms: *Okay*, *scram* and *You're telling me*. But some things never change, it seems, and it was also an era of massive unemployment with hunger marchers tramping south from Jarrow. King George V was on the throne and had been for nearly a quarter of a century.

Of the four grandchildren the King had at the time, the small girl at the upstairs window in Piccadilly was undeniably his favourite. He doted on her in a way he had never done on his own children. Nothing was too good

15

for her. He bought her her first pony; would send one of his royal carriages round to her Piccadilly home to take her for outings. When he went to Bognor to convalesce after illness, it was her he asked to have with him for company. Looking at each other through binoculars over the treetops of Green Park was a game they played often.

Her name, like his, was Windsor. It was a name she would have cause to use only once in her life; on the occasion of her marriage. Her first name was Elizabeth, though to avoid confusion with her mother, who was also Elizabeth, she was known as Lilibet in the family circle. Today she is known around the world as Queen Elizabeth II.

But no one in the early 1930s had any thought that she might one day be Queen. The direct line of succession ran not through her father, the King's second son, but through his elder brother, her Uncle David. And even for David kingship seemed so remote as to be unthinkable. To Britain and the Empire it seemed, at the time, as though the bearded father-figure of George V would reign for ever. Only his physicians and those close to him, like his wife May, knew that the fractured pelvis he had sustained when his horse rolled on him during a World War I visit to France still pained him and that he had never fully recovered from the two operations he had undergone in the late 1920s.

Outwardly George V, with his apple cheeks and booming quarter-deck voice, dapperly dressed in a frock coat and trousers which were carefully creased down the sides, continued to personify all that was immutable and enduring about Britain . . . all that was best in the British character . . . stolid, dignified, conscientious and hard working, totally moral in a way his father had never been, a man who was later remembered by his eldest son as believing firmly in 'God, the invincibility of the Royal Navy and the essential rightness of whatever was British.' So much the personification of Britain, of the English

16

character, that little Lilibet, when she needed to distinguish between him and her maternal Bowes-Lyon grandfather in Scotland, spoke of him as 'Grandpapa England'.

But while he may have been 'Grandpapa England' to his favourite grandchild, there was in fact very little that was pure English in George V's ancestry. His mother, the beautiful if eccentric Queen Alexandra, was Danish. His father, Edward VII, was so much the product of his own parents, Prince Albert of Saxe-Coburg-Gotha and Queen Victoria, with her Hanoverian antecedents, that he spoke English all his life with a slightly guttural inflection. For all that, Georgie, as his mother always called him, grew up so stolidly English in thought, word and deed that he was horrified to learn during World War I that it it was being whispered around that his heart was not really in the war effort because of the Germanic taint in his veins. Immediately he took steps to change his family name from Wettin, Wiper or whatever it was – strangely, no one was quite sure – to one with a stoutly British ring to it. The name he fixed upon was Windsor, after that castle on the Thames which had been the power base of England's kings since Saxon times.

Had his elder brother lived, George would probably never have become King. Certainly he would not have married Princess Victoria Mary of Teck and the whole course of family history would have been changed. But May, as she was called in the family, would still have become Queen Mary. Selected by George's father and grandmother, the matriarchal Queen Victoria, as having all the hallmarks of a future Queen, she was originally betrothed to the elder brother, the backward, unstable Albert Victor, Duke of Clarence.

Six weeks before they were to have been married, he died of pneumonia at Sandringham. George and May stood together in the bedroom doorway, comforting each other, as his life ebbed away. Eighteen months later, encouraged by that indefatigable matchmaker, George's grandmother, they were married. He was 'very fond' of her, Georgie told May, but 'not very much in love' with her.

Six children were born to them over the course of the next twelve years, five sons and a daughter. But the heartbreaking accidents of birth can as easily strike a royal family as any other family and, sadly, the youngest of the brood, John, was born an epileptic, subject to attacks so frequent and so violent that he was brought up apart from his brothers and sister in an isolated farmhouse on the family estate in Norfolk. He died there when barely into his teens.

John's death had already passed into family history when Lilibet was born in 1926. The remainder of George and Mary's brood were now grown up and two, Lilibet's father, Bertie, and her Aunt Mary, were married. Nevertheless, brothers and sister alike, in differing ways, bore the psychological scars of a not entirely successful upbringing at the hands of a disciplinarian father and a mother who was not over-endowed with the maternal instinct. Bertie, Mary and their younger brother, Harry, were alike shy, insecure and introspective. Bertie, in addition, was tormented with a nervous stammer. David, the eldest, if less shy and insecure than these three, was, by turns, headstrong and rebellious or moody and depressed. Only George, the youngest, seemed to have escaped the after-effects of a not always happy childhood. He was, at one and the same time, the most dashing and the most sensitive of the four surviving brothers, the most cultured and intellectual as he grew into manhood. Almost as though, some more distant members of the family were inclined to think at times, he came from a different strain altogether.

With the public at large, David, the straw-haired Prince of Wales, was the best-known and most popular, hailed and lauded as the blue-eyed boy of the British Empire as a result of his flag-showing cruises around the world during the 1920s. The constant adulation which came his way, both at home and overseas, was making him more and more self-willed and self-centred. Yet behind the crinkle-faced smile he wore in public there always lurked a sense of depression caused by the royal role in which he found himself cast.

'I'd give anything to change places with you,' he said more than once to his cousin, Dickie Mountbatten, who was in the Navy.

The two of them were close friends as well as cousins, often together at this early stage of their still-young lives. Having the more thrusting, more flamboyant Dickie around bolstered David's confidence, served as an antidote to his sense of insecurity. He took Dickie with him on several of his world tours and the younger cousin was perhaps the only one who saw David in tears because departure on each new trip involved an enforced separation from the mistress with whom he was so deeply in love at the time.

David had first met Freda, as he called her – Winifred Dudley Ward, a young married woman with two small children – during a 1918 air raid. She sought shelter at a house in Belgrave Square. There was a party going on in the house at the time and among the guests ushered down to join her in the protective shelter of the basement was the Prince of Wales, then twenty-four. He was immediately attracted to her, fell into conversation with her, persuaded her to stay on for the remainder of the party when the all-clear sounded and saw her home in the early hours of the morning. It was the start of a love affair which was to last some thirteen years. When David moved into his own bachelor establishment at the end of the war, Freda helped with the decor and furnishings. Years later, when he took over Fort Belvedere in 1930, she was still around to help plan the alterations and decorations. But he was not always faithful to her – there were always so many other attractive women eager to more than simply dance with the Prince of Wales – and by 1930 he was also involved in a more than casual relationship with Thelma Lady Furness.

If Dickie, in the 1920s, comforted David when royal duty tore him away from Freda's arms, David was quick to reciprocate when Dickie fell in love with Edwina Ashley, granddaughter of the multi-millionaire Ernest Cassel. Having already lost one girl while he was away with David in Australia and New Zealand, the young Mountbatten was fearful that Edwina would also find someone else while he was off to India and Japan. It was David who suggested to Dickie that he should invite her to join them in India.

Edwina had not yet come into her £7 million inheritance. A self-willed and impulsive young woman, she nevertheless borrowed £100 from an obliging aunt and paid her passage out to India. She and Dickie met up again in Delhi, where they became engaged, with the match-making David helping young love on its way by lending them the key to his private bungalow. When the two of them were married the following year, David served as Dickie's best man.

If David occasionally found his royal role depressing, Bertie, the second of the brothers, found it a downright ordeal on account of his stammer. Yet conscience compelled him to plug away at it dutifully, visiting so many mines, factories and shipyards that his brothers, who had once so cruelly mimicked his stammer, now teased him with the nickname of 'The Foreman'. Harry, the next eldest, every bit as shy and nervous as Bertie and Mary, also found the royal round a not inconsiderable ordeal. Sensibly, he decided to opt out of it as far as possible and took up a military career in the Hussars, though army duties were sometimes interrupted by the obligation to carry out royal duties. George, the youngest of the four, also decided that the royal round was not for him. Instead, he joined the Home Office and became an inspector of factories. 'The first civil servant in the family,' he joked about his job.

Of this second generation of Windsors, Mary had been the first to wed or, perhaps more accurately, to have been married off. She had little or no say in selecting the man she married. Her parents did the picking for her. Their choice fell upon 'Lucky' Lascelles, heir to the Earl of Harewood, a man fourteen years her senior, and she meekly acquiesced. If the age gap was not necessarily important, the difference in their temperaments did not augur well. While Mary was a shy, nervous girl, quiet and reserved, Lascelles was almost the exact opposite, a bluff, hearty character, very much a rough diamond of a man – insensitive to boot. Her parents were quite blind to this difference in temperaments. They saw it as a good match. Quite apart from the earldom he would one day inherit, Lascelles was already a wealthy man in his own right, having been left a £3 million fortune, by an eccentric Irish great-uncle. He was also a Master of Foxhounds, a member of the Jockey Club and had his own racing stable, attributes which Mary's father found suitably impressive.

David, in India at the time their engagement was announced, was less impressed. He saw clearly that the couple were unsuited and expressed himself as being 'not at all happy' about the whole affair. But David's views counted for little and Mary duly found herself led to the altar of Westminster Abbey. Once married, she was hauled off to the Harewood fastness in Yorkshire where 'Lucky', after fathering two sons, returned to his round of huntin', shootin' and racin', leaving his wife to seek solace from loneliness in a growing number of minor public engagements.

Even if Mary failed to find idyllic happiness in marriage, it was largely thanks to her that Bertie did so. One of the bridesmaids at her wedding was Elizabeth Bowes-Lyon, a small dainty girl with an infectious laugh and an irrepressible zest for living. Bertie was quite smitten with her and

21

various pretexts served to enable him to visit Glamis Castle in the Scottish Lowlands where she lived with her parents, the Earl and Countess of Strathmore and Kinghorne. The wonder was that he ever plucked up the courage to propose to her. Early childhood had long since knocked most of the confidence out of him. Frightened of his father, in awe of his mother, ignored almost to the point of neglect by his nanny, he had grown up so nervous and insecure that he would sit for hours in a darkened room rather than ask one of the servants to light a gas-mantle for him. Both he and Harry had inherited their father's knock-knees. In the hope of effecting a cure, their legs were clamped into splints which were so uncomfortable, even painful, that Harry was sometimes reduced to tears. Bertie was also born left-handed. Forced by his parents to use his right hand, the result was a nervous stammer which made him the butt of his brothers and sister.

In young manhood he still stammered when things got too much for him. But it was not this which caused Elizabeth Bowes-Lyon gently to reject him the first time he nerved himself to ask her to marry him. What troubled her was not his stammer, but the fact that he was the King's son. Marriage to him would also mean becoming one of the Royal Windsors. Never again, as she confided in a close friend, would she 'be free to think, speak or act as I really feel I should think, speak and act'.

Lacking in confidence though he may have been, Bertie was also persistent. The third time he proposed, Elizabeth accepted him. That she did so, she told a friend, was 'almost more of a surprise to me than it was to him'.

Bertie's parents were delighted with his choice. 'A lucky fellow', his father dubbed him. Elizabeth Bowes-Lyon was 'the one girl who could make Bertie happy', his mother said. And so it was to prove.

But if Bertie's marriage delighted them, the royal parents were concerned at the way their eldest son,

David, continued to kick his heels on the subject of marriage. They talked between themselves about the possibility of marrying him off to a foreign princess. However, foreign princesses were no longer so thick on the ground as they once had been and of the few eligible ones available, most of them were either too closely related or suspected of carrying the haemophilia handed down from Queen Victoria.

In any event, David was not another Mary to be meekly shepherded into a loveless match. Parental suggestions that it was his duty to marry and ensure the succession to the throne were brushed aside with a quizzical grin and a joking remark that 'Mary and Bertie have already done that'. With Freda and others prepared to go to bed with him without the benefit of his wedding ring on their fingers, marriage without love seemed a pointless exercise to him.

Morally, Bertie was a very different kettle of fish. If David was something of a throw-back to the laxer morals of their Hanoverian ancestors, Bertie had inherited the strait-laced attitude of their God-fearing disciplinarian father. From the first moment of meeting Elizabeth Bowes-Lyon he was never to love any other woman. And marriage to her was to be the making of him.

For all her earlier fears that she would never again be free to think, speak or act 'as I really feel I should think, speak and act', Elizabeth Bowes-Lyon did not allow marriage into the Royal Family to change her one jot. She remained the cheerful, warmly affectionate person she had always been, lively and with a 'quite delicious' sense of fun. It was the Royal Family which, under her influence, embarked upon a gradual process of change. Even her punctilious father-in-law, in her presence, became less gruff, more human. Lack of punctuality in anyone else would have driven him mad. Her he forgave. 'Must have sat down early,' he conceded readily when she and Bertie arrived late for a family dinner party one evening.

Bertie, at the time of his marriage, had given up hope of ever curing his stammer. Earlier he had worked hard and long at trying to conquer it, consulting specialist after specialist, embarking on one system of voice control after another. Nothing worked and each fresh failure left him more and more depressed.

It was shortly after marriage that someone mentioned the name of Lionel Logue, a speech therapist who was said to have worked wonders in his native Australia and was now in London. Bertie, at first, wanted nothing to do with Logue. It would only end in failure again, he said, and he did not think he could stand the disappointment of another failure. It was his wife, optimistic as always, who persuaded him that even a slight chance of success was worth the risk. 'Just one more try, darling,' she encouraged him.

She went with him to Logue's consulting rooms; worked with him on the system of exercises which Logue devised for her husband. She rehearsed Bertie's speeches with him until she knew them as well as he did and on public occasions her lips would move in accompaniment to his as she willed him through each new ordeal.

Initially, however, it seemed that he was to be proved right and she wrong. There was no improvement and Bertie became more depressed than ever. But she refused to be downcast; obstinately refused to admit defeat. 'We'll fight this together and we'll win,' she told him. He was still depressed, more apprehensive than ever, when they sailed together for Australia. At the end of the voyage lay the task of making the opening speech at Australia's first parliament – and he was dreading it.

Throughout the voyage, in the privacy of their cabin, she encouraged him to continue with the Logue system. Gradually the long hours of patient exercise paid off and there was far less sign of his longtime stammer when, keyed up and nervous, he finally delivered the all-important speech in Canberra. Impulsively, regardless of those around, she clutched his hand warmly. 'You were splendid, darling. I'm so proud of you.'

By that time Lilibet had been born. Grandpapa England was delighted that here at last was a grandchild with the family name of Windsor. Mary's two sons bore the Harewood family name of Lascelles. He fussed over the question of Christian names: Elizabeth Alexandra Mary. What about Victoria? Should not that be included also? Well, perhaps not.

But he put his foot down over the question of names when Elizabeth and Bertie had a second child, another daughter, some four years later. They wanted to call the new baby Ann Margaret. Grandpapa England did not care for the name Ann, he said. So Ann Margaret became Margaret Rose. She was more a bud than a rose, Lilibet said the first time she saw her baby sister.

Although the two girls had a nanny and a nursemaid to look after them in childhood, their mother personally supervised their upbringing in a way Gan Gan Queen Mary had never done with her children. She also kept a close eye on what went on in the kitchen, ensuring that Bertie's food was prepared in accordance with the diet he had been obliged to follow since being invalided out of the Navy in 1917 with duodenal ulcers. Indeed, in every respect possible she brought to their family life the same warmth and happiness she had known throughout her own childhood . . . so that, looking back years later, her elder daughter was to recall those formative years at 145 Piccadilly as a time 'when the sun always seemed to be shining'. In reality, of course, there was no more sunshine then than today. Perhaps less in a coal-burning era when London knew more smog. In those days, bathnight for Lilibet and Margaret meant a tin tub in front of the nursery fire with coal and hot water alike hauled all the way up from the basement. The ever-shining sun which Queen Elizabeth II still recalls all these years later was the brightness of her mother's personality and the affectionate family atmosphere she wove around her.

Wife and husband alike were homebodies, eschewing the gadabout social life favoured by many of their friends. They might occasionally pop out together of an evening to go to the talkies at Marble Arch, but usually they stayed home, playing simple card games like Snap and Happy Families with their two small daughters and then, when nanny had taken the girls up to bed, settling down together to listen to the wireless, with Bertie popping along to the kitchen later to prepare a nightcap of hot cocoa.

The occasional relatives would pop in from time to time, Mary and her two sons, George and Gerald, or Bertie's elder brother, David. He was Lilibet and Margaret's favourite uncle, joining in their games, thoroughly enjoying the simple pleasures of family life which were in such striking contrast to his own more sophisticated mode of living. Sometimes he would turn up bearing gifts brought back from his foreign travels and for Lilibet's birthday one year he bought her her first puppy. 'A happy home', David thought it, perhaps a shade enviously, with his brother possessed of 'a matchless blessing' in such a wife and two such lovely daughters. David and his Bowes-Lyon sister-in-law, in the years before Mrs Simpson came to obsess him, were the best of friends.

Just as the Queen remembers her childhood as a time when the sun always seemed to be shining, so her mother was always to look back on the five years which followed Margaret's birth, with Lilibet a child still, as a particularly golden age. Her fears about what marriage into the Royal Family would involve had proved unfounded, Bertie's stammer had been almost vanquished and her brother-in-law's future abdication was still unthought of.

There were summer holidays at Balmoral with Grandpapa England and Gan Gan; old-fashioned Christmases at Sandringham. If Lilibet and Margaret thought it great fun when Grandpapa came down to breakfast with his pet parrot perched on his hand, turning the bird loose to strut among the breakfast things, not everyone was so amused.

But best of all were the weekends at Royal Lodge, a rather run-down rural retreat in Windsor Great Park which Grandpapa England gave to his son and daughter-in-law in the early 1930s. Shabby though it was, they were delighted with it and promptly set to work to restore and re-model it. While builders worked on the house itself, Bertie and Elizabeth set about tackling the garden. Years of neglect had turned it into something of a wilderness and reclaiming it, Elizabeth thought, would not only be good for Bertie's always uncertain health but also serve as an antidote to the stress and strain he experienced in public life. Bertie promptly press-ganged everyone else into helping out, equerry, valet, butler, chauffeur and detective, plus any friends or relatives who chanced to call. While the grown-ups hacked and slashed at the overgrown shrubberies with billhooks and pruning knives, the two girls, once they were old enough, collected the prunings and piled them into what became a series of large, smoky bonfires. Their mother followed on behind, her green fingers doing the planting, creating a rose garden and flowerbeds where there had once been wilderness.

Bertie became inordinately proud of the garden as it took shape. 'This really is my garden,' he would tell visitors. 'I made it myself.' His smiling wife was more than happy for him to take the credit.

2

Enter Wallis

A few miles from Royal Lodge, the eldest of the four sons of Grandpapa England spent his weekends in very different style from the way in which Bertie and Elizabeth spent theirs. Life within the mock battlements of a Georgian folly named Fort Belvedere – David always referred to it casually as 'The Fort' – was far more elegant and sophisticated, in keeping with its princely owner's very different attitude to life and living. The unhappy childhood which hád made Bertie so uncertain and insecure had had the reverse effect upon David, making him self-willed and rebellious. So far it was rebellion in only a minor-key, revealing itself in such unroyal standards of dress as two-tone shoes and check suits more suited to a bookmaker or music-hall comic than a Prince of Wales. While Bertie and Elizabeth found pleasure in winning back their garden, David lived life at a faster pace, surrounding himself with bright young things of his own generation, handing round newfangled American concoctions called 'cocktails' and, if the mood was upon him, entertaining them with snatches on his ukelele or bagpipes. Among his guests one weekend at the Fort, with its pine panelling, Chippendale furniture and paintings by Canaletto, were the Ernest Simpsons.

By the strict, and perhaps rather prudish, standards of the day, the Simpsons should have had no place in the royal circle. Husband and wife had both been previously married and divorced, and neither David's father nor his brothers would have had them as house guests for that reason. David himself was strangely fascinated by anything American – cocktails, clothes, jazz – and the Simpsons were American, Ernest Simpson on his mother's side only, his wife on both sides of her family tree. Her father, she liked to say, was a Warfield of Maryland and her mother a Montague of Virginia. It was the wife, a dominantly elegant woman in her mid-thirties to whom David, thirty-seven at this time, was especially attracted. He had first met her when, soon after returning from a tour of South America, he had popped round to see his latest light o' love, Thelma Lady Furness, and found a cocktail party in progress.

'This is Wallis,' Thelma had said, introducing them. 'She's just over from the States.'

At birth, in fact, following the practice common in the southern states of America, she had been given the double-barrelled name of Bessie-Wallis, but had later dropped the old-fashioned Bessie while retaining the more elegant Wallis. At twenty, eager to get away from home, she had married a young officer in the US Navy Air Corps, Earl Winfield Spencer Jr. It proved to be a tempestuous relationship. She flirted and he punished her by locking her in the bathroom. There were separations and reconciliations. Finally, in 1927, they were divorced and the following year she married Ernest Simpson, who was also divorced. They moved to Britain when he transferred to the London office of his father's firm.

David first invited the Simpsons to the Fort for a winter weekend in the January of 1932. They were invited several more times that year and the following year, when Wallis celebrated her thirty-seventh birthday, David gave a party for her at Quaglino's. After that, the Simpsons were at the Fort nearly every weekend. Then, early in 1934, Thelma decided on a trip to the States to visit her twin sister, Gloria Vanderbilt.

'Look after the little man for me,' she said to Wallis. 'See that he doesn't get into any mischief.'

David telephoned Thelma frequently while she was away; sent her lovey-dovey cables in their private code. But he was also popping round to Bryanston Square to see Wallis, with her husband sometimes retreating into his study to work, leaving them alone. By the time Thelma returned to London, his feelings for her had undergone a change. She sensed it the moment they met again and had a shrewd suspicion that Wallis, though she denied it, was the cause. Suspicion became certainty that weekend at the Fort as she saw the meaningful glances which passed between them. Late that night, when she and David were alone, she asked him pointblank if he was 'keen' on Wallis.

'Don't be silly,' he told her. The way he said it lacked conviction and the following morning Thelma re-packed her things, left the Fort and passed out of his life.

In his infatuation for Wallis, David was ruthless in cutting old ties. During his long relationship with Freda Dudley Ward he had always displayed almost fatherly concern and affection for her two daughters. Now all at once, with one of them very ill, he neither called nor telephoned to inquire how she was coming along. Surprised and puzzled, Freda tried to telephone him . . . only to be told by the operator at St James's Palace, 'I am sorry, but I have orders not to put you through.'

He began escorting Wallis to nightclubs. She became an obligatory guest at weekend house parties to which he was invited. With her aunt, Bessie Merryman, along as chaperon, he took her on holiday to Biarritz. While there, they went cruising on Lord Moyne's yacht, *Rosaurus*. Though Wallis has always denied that she was ever David's mistress, she has also confessed that it was aboard *Rosaurus* that their relationship 'crossed the boundary between friendship and love'.

Arrogant and self-willed though he could often be with

others, with her he was like a little lapdog, meekly trotting off in search of a piece of emery board if she so much as chipped her nail varnish, inundating her with expensive gifts. He bought her a necklace from Cartier of Paris and bedecked her with other jewels which, strictly speaking, were not his to give. True, they had been left to him by his grandmother, Queen Alexandra, who died in 1925, but this was on the assumption that they would one day adorn another Princess of Wales. In a word – and the word was used by George, youngest of the four royal brothers and the closest to David in terms of brotherly love – he was 'besotted' with the woman.

George, at that time, was excellently placed to form a judgement. He was in love himself. The object of his affections was Princess Marina, the elegantly beautiful daughter of Prince Nicholas of Greece, a tall, willowy young woman with most unusual eyes, brown with a surrounding ring of grey-green. 'Trout's eyes', her father teased her. Like so many other Greek royals of the period, her cousin Prince Philip among them, hers had been an unsettled upbringing, dodging back and forth into exile in Switzerland, England, France, as Greece discarded monarchy, reinstated it, shed it again. It was in Paris, where money was so scarce that she made many of her own clothes, that she gained her flair for fashion. Her two older sisters, Olga and Elizabeth, had both married, but she herself seemed in no hurry. She was waiting for a man she could really love, she said.

She met him finally in London, at one of a number of parties to which she was invited. For George too it was love at first sight. Well, almost. He took her to the pictures, for walks in Green Park, for drives in his car. His fast driving did not worry her. Both were athletic, though she generally had the best of it at tennis. More importantly, as George said, 'We laugh at the same things.' Then royal duty required him to visit South Africa while Marina returned to her Parisian home in exile.

Back home again, George arranged for her to be invited to Cowes for the yachting and went there hoping to meet her again. She did not turn up. Inquiries revealed that she was staying with her sister Olga and brother-in-law Paul at their chalet at Bohinj in Slovenia. George was always the most impulsive of the brothers and, pricked into realisation by her absence, he asked David for the loan of his private airplane. Of the brothers, they – the youngest and eldest – were the closest and David was always generous where George was concerned. Earlier, when their father had refused George the money to buy a car, David had bought him a brand-new Wolseley. 'Help yourself,' he said now.

George cancelled his outstanding engagements, sent a telegram to announce his coming and flew to Yugoslavia, following so quickly on the telegram that there was no one at the aerodrome to greet him. He hired a car and drove out to the chalet. It s pinewood, flower-filled setting was idyllic for young love. For the next five days George and Marina were constantly together, walking in the woods, swimming in the lake, sun-bathing, playing tennis and back-gammon. On the fifth night, Marina's uncle, Prince Christopher, who was also staying at the chalet, found himself dying for a smoke at bedtime. But he had left his cigarette case downstairs. He put on his dressing gown and went in search of it. Though everyone else had gone to bed, George and Marina were still in the sitting room, in each other's arms, so engrossed they did not hear the door open. Uncle Christopher withdrew quietly and went to bed that night without his customary last cigarette.

They were married in London, at Westminster Abbey, on a cold, damp November day in 1934. David was best man. Bertie went with him to York House to collect the bridegroom on his wedding morning. They were amazed to find him pushing his way through the vast crowd gathered outside.

'Where on earth have you been?' they demanded almost in unison once all three were safely inside again.

'To the bank,' George replied, cheerfully. He had found himself short of cash for his honeymoon, he explained, so he had walked to his bank in the Strand and cashed a cheque.

Lilibet was one of the bride's youthful train-bearers at a wedding which, like Prince Charles's wedding nearly half-a-century later, brought a welcome touch of glamour to a country sunk deep in depression. Hunger-marchers had tramped south to London earlier that same year, yet no one seemed to envy the Royals their wedding splash. There were a few ribald jokes, but in good spirit. Uncle Christopher heard one.

Why will Princess Marina make things smooth for Prince George? Because she's been preserved in Greece.

Christopher passed it on to the bridegroom's father, who loved a good joke. Next day, at the wedding reception, guests were all repeating it to each other.

The only small blot on the wedding came not from the unemployed, but through David. He added the names of Mr and Mrs Ernest Simpson to the guest list for a celebration ball. His father spotted the addition and crossed the names out again. David was furious. So furious that he bearded his father on the matter. Uncharacteristically, George V gave way. The names were added again to the guest list and Wallis went to the ball. Not only that, but David insisted on presenting her to his parents.

The married lifestyle of George and Marina was to prove very different from that of Bertie and Elizabeth. Bertie and Elizabeth were homebodies; George and Marina were intellectuals. Their London residence in Belgrave Square and their country home, Coppins, a gabled farmhouse left to them by the unmarried Princess Victoria, George's aunt and Marina's godmother, quickly became meeting places for musicians, artists, writers, actors. The Fairbankses, the Oliviers, Noel Coward and Malcolm Sargeant were among their friends. Marina quickly became a leader of fashion. Her pillbox 'Marina hats' and her favourite colour – 'Marina blue' – became all the rage. She turned all this to the national advantage, popularising Lancashire cotton (on George's suggestion), Nottingham lace, Scottish tweed.

Shortly after George's wedding, Ernest Simpson found it necessary to go to New York on business. He wanted Wallis to go with him, but she refused. Instead, she went to Kitzbuehel on a ski-ing holiday with David and on to Vienna and Budapest.

Queen Mary had long since given up hope of persuading David to marry and settle down. So now, with Mary, Bertie and George all safely married, she turned her attention to Harry. 'You will have to follow suit,' she told him at the time of George's wedding and supplied the names of two princesses she felt might be suitable. Grandpapa England added his weight. 'Mama and I have always been anxious that you should marry and settle down,' he wrote to Harry soon after.

Harry, nudging thirty-five, was perhaps more encouraged by a meeting with brother George and his new bride. They were on honeymoon in the West Indies and his path crossed theirs as he returned from a royal tour of Australia and New Zealand. Until now, he had been by no means anxious to marry, feeling that marriage might hinder his career in the army. Bachelors, he had noted, seemed to be given preference over married men when it came to the question of appointing commanding officers. However, promotion suddenly seemed of less importance and within weeks of returning home Harry was courting, not one of the princesses advocated by his mother, but a young woman with a quiet, retiring disposition to match his own, Alice Montagu-Douglas-Scott, sister of his long-time friend, Lord William Scott.

That was in 1935, the year of Grandpapa England's silver jubilee. With her parents and sister Margaret, Lilibet, now nine, headed the carriage procession as the King drove through London to a thanksgiving service in

St Paul's Cathedral. As on the occasion of George's wedding, huge crowds cheered the family every yard of the way. Grandpapa England, normally a rather unemotional man, was for once stirred by it all, if a little bemused also. 'I don't understand it,' he said. 'I'm only a very ordinary fellow. You know, I'm beginning to think they really must like me for myself.'

Surprised and delighted though he was by his evident popularity, he was also concerned that the family's standing in public opinion might be undermined by any further spate of royal spending on top of George's wedding and his own silver jubilee junket. So, anxious though he was for Harry to marry, he hesitated momentarily when his third son sought formal permission, necessary despite his age because of his position in relation to the succession to the throne, to wed Alice. David did not require his father's permission before taking Wallis off on yet another European jaunt, this time to Cannes with a couple of Mediterranean cruises thrown in for good measure.

In Cannes David met up with cousin Dickie and his wife Edwina. They had been married now for some thirteen years and were parents twice over. On the surface, theirs was a happy, exciting, spendthrift marriage, but behind the scenes married life was not always smooth sailing. Edwina was impulsive, volatile, headstrong, and with an enormous fortune at her command. She could indulge her slightest whim . . . whims which sometimes took rather odd forms. Later she was to divert her tremendous zest and energy into more meaningful directions, but in those early days of marriage she would sometimes take off at little more than a moment's notice . . . sailing around the Polynesian islands in a trading schooner, travelling across Russia on the trans-Siberian railway, going on an archaeological dig in Persia, driving the length of Africa in a car. If Dickie, for all his own flamboyance, sometimes found this sort of thing difficult, there were, in addition, her occasional friendships with other men which hurt him more. But the stresses in their marriage were well concealed as they went around with David and Wallis in a convivial foursome.

As things turned out, there was to be no great splash for Harry and Alice's wedding as there had been with George and Marina. Three weeks before the couple were to be married, Alice's father, the Duke of Buccleuch, died. Every reason to cancel the bulk of the wedding invitations which had been sent out earlier. Instead of two thousand guests in Westminster Abbey, there were fewer than two hundred in the private chapel at Buckingham Palace. With little liking for the ostentation of the grand occasion, both Harry and Alice found the smaller, quieter ceremony infinitely more to their taste. Lilibet was again one of the bride's attendants, reinforced this time by sister Margo, considered old enough now that she was five not to let the family down on formal occasions.

Grandpapa England had now reached the allotted biblical span of three score years and ten and his health, never very good in recent years, was failing fast. As conscientious and dutiful as ever, he not only plugged away at his work as usual but worried about what would happen to the country when he was gone. He had little faith in David's ability to step into his shoes. 'After I'm gone, that boy will ruin himself in twelve months,' he said on one occasion. It was to prove an uncannily accurate prophecy.

To George V, Sandringham had always been, 'the place I love better than anywhere else in the world'. As newlyweds, he and May had set up home there, squeezing their fast-growing family into the small cramped villa his father gave them as a wedding gift, so small that the smell of cooking in the kitchen tended to permeate the whole place. With the exception of David, all their children had been born there. Even after becoming King and Queen, the two of them had continued to live at

Sandringham whenever they could escape from London. With the death of George's mother in 1925, they had moved from the villa into the spaciousness of the 'big house' and it had become their custom to surround themselves with their children and grandchildren each Christmas.

But that Christmas of 1935 was slightly unusual in several respects. Bertie and Elizabeth were unable to journey to Sandringham because Elizabeth was down with flu. However, the two girls, Elizabeth and Margo, went to be with their grandparents for Christmas. George now had not only a wife, but a baby son, Eddy, born in the October, and it gave Grandpapa England pleasure, that last Christmas of his life, to watch the nipper being bathed.

As Christmas became New Year, the King's health was clearly deteriorating fast. Worried about him, some of the family stayed on at Sandringham longer than usual. Others left, but returned hurriedly as his condition rapidly worsened. David flew there in his private airplane as it became increasingly clear that his father had not long to live. Bertie was summoned from Royal Lodge, where Elizabeth was abed with flu.

'Feel rotten,' the King noted shakily in his diary on 17 January after his physician, Lord Dawson, had examined him yet again.

For years, his diaries and his stamp collection, along with his shooting, had been the great passions of his otherwise rather passionless life. He had started collecting stamps at the age of twenty-five, when he was in the Navy, and had continued to devote three afternoons a week to his collection even after becoming King. Now, forty-five years later it filled a staggering 325 volumes. He had started his diary-keeping even earlier, as a fifteen-year-old naval cadet. Year by year he had filled diary after diary, assiduously, meticulously . . . until now.

The entry he made following Lord Dawson's visit on 17

January was to be the last in his own hand. And even that was incomplete. He was too weak to hold his pen any longer and May had to take over for him.

They had been married for nearly forty-three years. Theirs was a marriage bred of convenience out of the shared sorrow over Albert Victor's death. Failures as parents however successful they may have been as King and Queen, husband and wife were alike inhibited to the point where they sometimes found it easier to write notes to each other than to speak of their feelings. Yet even if their marriage never knew the warmth their second son was to find in his marriage to Elizabeth Bowes-Lyon, there nevertheless developed between them a loyalty, companionship and sense of dependence upon each other which stood the test of time. It lasted until 20 January 1936, when, as May wrote in the diary Grandpapa England had been unable to continue: 'My dearest husband, King Geo. V . . . passed away at 5 minutes before midnight.'

3

Exit Uncle David

It had been one of Grandpapa England's foibles, copied from his father before him, always to have the clocks at Sandringham set half an hour ahead of the rest of the country. Another was to order his carriage round at odd times . . . three minutes to the hour or seven minutes past. This ensured that the carriage arrived punctually, he said.

There was similar reasoning behind the matter of the clocks. The idea was to get house guests at Sandringham out of their beds and the men out with their guns half an hour earlier, thus giving them an extra half-hour of daylight in winter during which to blast away at pheasants and partridges.

Even the clock on the parish church in Sandringham Park was set half an hour ahead of the rest of Britain! 'Sandringham time', the dead King had termed it. If some people thought the idea ingenious while others found it mildly amusing, there were yet others to whom it had long been an irritant. David in particular. It irritated him, telephoning Wallis from Sandringham, to have her tell him that it was actually a half-hour earlier than he imagined, and when Sandringham's unique system of timekeeping caused yet another muddle for him on the night his father lay dying, he lost patience entirely. For all that he was not yet King and master of Sandringham, he

39

gave orders for the clocks to be altered to the correct time. A telephone call alerted a clockmaker in nearby King's Lynn and he set out for Sandringham. By the time he got there George V was dead and Edward VIII reigned in his place. Almost the first action Queen Mary made was to curtsey to the son who was now King and kiss his hand.

From Sandringham, the body of Grandpapa England was taken to London for its lying in state. The Royal Standard was draped over the coffin and the Imperial Crown perched on top as it was drawn on a gun carriage from King's Cross station to Westminster Hall. The jolting of the gun carriage caused the the Maltese cross atop the crown to fall off. It was hastily scooped up by a sergeant-major of the Grenadiers. David, following behind the coffin with his brothers, was a witness to the incident.

'Although not superstitious, I wondered whether it was a bad omen,' he noted later.

The order of succession to the throne descends vertically in the first place, with males taking precedence over females, and horizontally only secondarily. In David's case, because he was unmarried and childless, it could not descend vertically. So the horizontal took over, making his brother Bertie the next in line. Bertie did have children of course, Lilibet and Margo, and they ranked next, ahead of their uncles, David and Bertie's younger brothers, Harry and George.

The two girls had been returned to Royal Lodge from Sandringham once it became clear that Grandpapa England was dying. 'Don't let all this depress them more than is absolutely necessary,' their mother instructed governess Marion Crawford. All the same, it was deemed necessary for Lilibet, for all that she was not yet ten, to be garbed in black and taken to see Grandpapa England lying in state. 'Everyone was so quiet,' she told Miss Crawford when she got back. 'As if the King were asleep.'

Any hopes the rest of the family may have had that David's infatuation with Wallis would magically cease now that he was King were speedily to be dashed. On the contrary, he seemed more besotted with her than ever and his mother, his brothers and their wives felt a fresh sense of dismay when they learned that he had had her with him at St James's Palace, standing with her at a window, to watch the ceremony of his proclamation. Nor were the family the only ones who knew of and were troubled by the continuing, and growing, relationship. There was an occasion when an appointment with prime minister Stanley Baldwin was delayed somewhat because the King had popped over to see Wallis. When he discovered the cause of the delay, Baldwin was both offended and perturbed.

Had David been content to take Wallis as his mistress, had she been content to accept that role, there would have been no problem. The hypocrisy of the age would have tolerated a King with a mistress provided the fact was not publicly paraded. But David was more and more set on the idea of marrying her, while she, for all her laughing denials when friends quizzed her, was perhaps equally delighted with the idea of marrying him. She saw no problem once she was divorced from Ernest Simpson. David was King and the King was all-powerful. David himself knew that it was not going to be that easy. He had need of allies, inside and outside the family. Close as they had always been, he felt that his youngest brother, George, would be on his side if it came to the crunch. Now he set about winning over Bertie and his laughing, likeable little wife.

With this in mind, he drove over one day from the Fort to Bertie's weekend retreat at Royal Lodge. The ostensible purpose of the trip was to show his brother the glossy new American station wagon (or shooting brake) he had recently acquired. But the true purpose was to bring Wallis and Elizabeth together in the hope that friendship would spark between them. It didn't work out like that.

Bertie and Elizabeth duly admired David's new car. He

took Bertie for a short drive in it. The four of them strolled round the garden, talking of this and that, but it was a stilted, awkward conversation. Afterwards they had tea in the drawing room where the children, Lilibet and Margaret, joined them. It was not a comfortable occasion. David, intent on winning his brother and sister-in-law over, was rather offhand for once with their two small daughters. They, in turn, were rather put out by the excessive amount of jewellery which Uncle David's lady friend had on display, by her dominant manner and brittle American accent. 'Who is she?' Lilibet wanted to know. Bertie said very little; he was never much of a talker and found the whole situation slightly uncomfortable. His wife chatted away as animatedly as always, but Wallis nevertheless gained the impression that she didn't really like her. In that, she was undoubtedly correct. There was a possessiveness about her attitude to David which his brother and sister-in-law both instinctively resented. They may also have sensed that David had an ulterior motive for his seemingly casual call on them.

Later, after Wallis was divorced, David tried to ensure the support of George and Marina in a similar fashion, by taking Wallis to visit them. He obtained little more satisfaction from that visit to Coppins than he had done at Royal Lodge. Left to their own devices, both Bertie and George might have been more tolerant in the view they took of his lady-love, but they took their cues from their wives and Marina had no more liking for Wallis than Elizabeth had.

Undeterred by his failure to gain family support, David forged ahead obstinately to have Wallis accepted by the country of which he was now King. He invited her and her husband to dine with him at Buckingham Palace and saw to it that their names appeared in the court circular as having done so. He had Wallis to dine at the palace a second time, this time without her husband, and again had the fact published in the court circular. In a further attempt to win over Bertie and Elizabeth to his side, he invited them to the same dinner party. That evening, Wallis went out of her way to ingratiate herself with the King's sister-in-law, doing her best to subdue her own powerful personality, but without success.

Step by step, events moved inexorably towards the crisis which was to split the family for more than a generation. Wallis parted from her husband and moved into a new and larger apartment in Regent's Park, with David sending round various items from the palace, even blankets, to help her furnish it. He had her and a number of her friends to stay with him at Balmoral, where she upset some of the staff by acting as though she was already mistress of the place. Bertie and Elizabeth were staying nearby, at Birkhall, at the same time and David asked his brother if he would mind deputising for him at the opening ceremony of a new hospital in Aberdeen. Bertie did so willingly enough, but was upset and indignant when he discovered later that David had backed out of the ceremony simply in order to collect Wallis from the station when she arrived from London and drive her personally to Balmoral. That, in Bertie's view, was no way for a King to behave.

There were other aspects of David's attitude, as both King and brother, which equally troubled Bertie. He was particularly disturbed by his brother's view that Sandringham was an expensive white elephant. Either the cost of running the place must be drastically cut, David insisted, or it would have to be sold. Bertie could hardly deny that Sandringham, the way it had been run under their father, had been a considerable extravagance. All the same, it had been the dead King's favourite retreat and Bertie felt it was a bit soon after his death to be talking of selling a place which had been so close to his father's heart. David took no such sentimental view. He did not care for Sandringham, never had, and during the short time he was on the throne went there only once more, using it as a temporary base from which to visit Wallis while she was domiciled in Felixstowe as a necessary prelude to her divorce.

That summer David and Wallis went cruising together. David chartered the luxury yacht *Nahlin* from Lady Yule for a dawdle along the Dalmatian coast. He had the somewhat naïve idea that if he styled himself Duke of Lancaster wherever he went, the whole affair would pass off unnoticed by the world at large. Of course it did not. He could no more conceal his true identity than he could any longer conceal his true feelings for Wallis even in public. Crowds flocked to gape at the pair of them whenever they ventured ashore, press cameras clicked busily and reporters cabled stories of their togetherness to newspapers around the world. Some of the photographs showed the so-called Duke of Lancaster wearing nothing more than shorts and sandals while others revealed him and Wallis in poses which spoke volumes of their true relationship.

Neither photographs nor stories appeared in Britain's newspapers, more circumspect then than now about intruding into the private lives of the Royal Family. But David's mother and brothers, as well as people like Baldwin, received letters and cuttings from abroad which increased their concern. They derived comfort from the fact that Wallis, though separated from her husband, was still legally Mrs Ernest Simpson. While that continued to be the case, David, infatuated though he might be with her, could not possibly marry her. Then came news which shattered even this fond hope. Wallis was planning to sue for divorce.

David's mother and brothers were horrified. Now all their worst fears were moving towards realisation. There could be no doubt that David was hoping to marry Wallis once she was free . . . to make her, a twice-divorced woman, his Queen. The idea was unthinkable. Yet they were powerless to do anything about it. Headstrong and self-opiniated as he was, infatuated as he was, he would brook no argument, no opposition.

But if the family felt they could do nothing, Baldwin saw it as his duty, as prime minister, to intervene and made an appointment to see David at Fort Belvedere. His plea for the King to persuade 'the lady' not to go through with her divorce was met with haughty refusal. It was the lady's private business, David told him, curtly, in which he (the King) had no right to interfere.

'No desire' might have been nearer the exact truth. David could, and did, interfere in other ways. A little string-pulling on his part resulted in the divorce being heard not in London but in the quiet East Anglian backwater of Ipswich, where it might perhaps attract less publicity.

The divorce petition was brought on the grounds that Ernest Simpson had committed adultery. It was the fashion of the day for the husband to accept the blame in such cases and Ernest duly complied to the extent of furnishing evidence that he had spent the night at an hotel in Bray with a lady possessing the fanciful name of Buttercup Kennedy.

Britain's newspapers continued to treat the whole business with the utmost discretion, restricting their report of the case to no more than a few lines. And no mention of the King, of course. In America things were very different. There, even before the case had been heard, at least one newspaper was headlining the fact that Britain's King Edward VIII planned to marry America's Wallis Simpson once she had been divorced for the second time.

The divorce was granted on 27 October, though under the law of those days it would not become final for another six months. This still left time for David and Wallis to marry before his coronation, planned for the following May.

It was to be another three weeks before David confirmed the family's worst fears and told them that it was his definite intention to marry Wallis. They already knew, of

45

course; had known for some time. Indeed, Bertie, with his wife's help, after trying in vain to see his brother, had written him a letter of personal appeal. He wanted David to be happy, he said in the letter, and understood his feelings, but urged him to consider the best interests of the country and the Empire.

It did no good. David was deaf to all reason. More infatuated with Wallis than ever, accustomed to others deferring to him and always getting his own way, he saw no reason why he should not get it in the matter of marriage also, and on 16 November he telephoned Marlborough House to arrange a meeting with his mother. She suggested that he should have dinner with her that evening. Mary, his sister, was in London at the time and he asked his mother to invite her also. To his surprise, when he arrived at Marlborough House that evening, there was yet another guest for dinner, his sister-in-law Alice, Harry's wife. Her presence was unexpected and unforeseen, and David had too much sense of family to permit his brother to learn what was in his mind through a second party. So after dinner he asked Alice to excuse them and he, his mother and sister adjourned to Queen Mary's boudoir with its cluttered bric-à-brac – someone once counted ninety pieces on the large rosewood writing table alone – and its dominating portrait of his dead father, Grandpapa England.

Bracing himself, he told his mother and sister what he had already told Baldwin, the prime minister, earlier that evening. He intended to marry Wallis as soon as her divorce was made absolute. If he could marry her as King, all well and good. If not, then he would abdicate.

'Well, this is a pretty kettle of fish,' said his mother.

'Very painful', said his sister. 'A terrible blow.'

His mother asked him to think again; not to shirk his duty as King. 'You have my true sympathy,' she told him, 'but I implore you, for the sake of the family and the sake of the country, not to abdicate.' She urged him to give Wallis up.

'Let me bring her to see you?' David begged.

His mother was shocked and angered by the idea. It was 'deeply humiliating', she said.

This provoked David into a petulant, almost hysterical, outburst. 'I can't do my job without her. I am going to marry her, and I will.'

'Really, this might be Rumania,' said Queen Mary, haughtily.

There was a similar harrowing scene the following day when David convened a meeting of his three brothers and told them what he planned. Of the three, George was perhaps the most understanding and sympathetic. Harry seemed more concerned with how far abdication, if it took place, would affect his own position and his army career. Bertie, the one who would be most affected if his brother did abdicate, was too shocked by the whole business to say anything.

The vast majority of the public still knew nothing of this grave emotional crisis at the very heart of the nation. An outward appearance of normality in royal life was maintained with a continuing round of public duties. A spate of such duties took Bertie and Elizabeth north to Scotland towards the end of November. While they were away rumours of a Guy Fawkes type plot to blow up Wallis' house, and her with it, came to David's ears. Nothing would satisfy him but she must pack her things and let him drive her to the Fort. Her Aunt Bessie came along as chaperone.

Bertie and Elizabeth returned to London early in December to be greeted by newspaper placards concerning THE KING'S MARRIAGE when their overnight train steamed into Euston station. The story had finally broken in Britain. David's love for Wallis was no longer simply a family affair, but a national crisis. Bertie was 'horrified'. The two of them went to Marlborough House that evening to have dinner with Queen Mary. She was 'aghast', she said. 'What about David?' Bertie asked. She had not seen

47

hair nor hide of him for ten days, Queen Mary replied, but she had asked him to join them that evening.

David showed up very late. He looked tense and was clearly under very considerable strain. In fact, he had not long since said goodbye to Wallis. After earlier turning down a suggestion that she should leave the country until the whole situation was resolved one way or the other, he had finally decided that, with feelings running so high, she would be safer out of the way. But he was still determined to marry her, he said. 'I cannot live alone as King. I must marry her.'

Even at this eleventh hour Bertie still had hopes that he might persuade his brother to change his mind. They must talk, he said. 'Come and see me at the Fort tomorrow,' David told him. But when Bertie rang him the following morning, he put him off. It would have to be the next day, he said now.

The next day Bertie and Elizabeth drove to Royal Lodge for the weekend as usual. From there Bertie telephoned David again – and again David put him off. 'Come tomorrow – Sunday,' he said. On Sunday Bertie telephoned his brother again, only to be told that the King was engaged and would call him back. No call came.

David was in such a state of mental conflict that he scarcely knew what he was doing. Personally he considered his cause lost and wanted only to go; but others were still urging him to stay and fight it out. Wallis especially. Long, insistent telephone calls from her in Cannes – 'You are the King, David. Your popularity will carry you through' – brought him almost to the verge of breakdown.

The two brothers finally met on Monday evening. Both were tired, strained and on edge. Bertie reiterated his earlier arguments . . . *think of the country and the Empire.* David interrupted him almost before he had started. He had made up his mind, he said. He was definitely going to abdicate. Bertie felt terrible. Until now he had not permitted himself to face up to what was involved. But now he had to and the prospect appalled him. Painfully shy as he was, with his stammer, poor health, complete lack of training, how could he ever be King?

'This is absolutely terrible,' he told Elizabeth on his return home. 'I never wanted this to happen. David has been trained for this all his life. I have never even seen a state paper.'

There were some people in high places who shared his doubts. They would have preferred to pass over both Bertie and Harry, who was almost as shy and unsure of himself as Bertie, and settle for the youngest brother, the more dashing George, as the next King. Besides, they argued, George already had a son to succeed him while Bertie had only daughters. Some newspapers echoed these sentiments, to Bertie's distress. 'They don't want me,' he said, despairingly, after reading the papers.

His wife did her best to buoy and sustain his spirits. 'We must take what is coming to us and make the best of it,' she said, fatalistically.

Bertie was further heartened by a meeting with his cousin, Dickie Mountbatten. The flamboyant, supremely confident Dickie saw no problem at all in what lay ahead for Bertie.

'I am only a naval officer,' Bertie said. In fact, it was nearly twenty years since he had been invalided out. 'It's the only thing I know anything about.'

'What a curious coincidence,' his cousin replied. 'I remember my father telling me that your father, when the Duke of Clarence died, said almost the same thing to him. And my father answered, "George, you are wrong. There is no more fitting preparation for a king than to have been trained in the navy."'

Bertie was close to tears as he spoke with his cousin. Visiting his mother at Marlborough House some time later, he completely broke down and sobbed on her shoulder like a child. But he was very much in command of himself and his emotions on 10 December when, along with Harry and George, he witnessed David's signing of the Instrument of Abdication. In fact, because David could no longer be bothered, he had been dealing with affairs of state for a day or two already, although it was not until the next day, when Parliament ratified his brother's abdication, that he actually became King. Not King Albert (though the dead Queen Victoria would have liked that). In an attempt to paper over the cracks caused by the abdication, he decided to take his father's name and become King George VI. He hoped that time would enable him 'to make amends for what has happened', he told Stanley Baldwin. Now that the die was cast, he seemed determined if not fully confident. It was his wife, after staunchly supporting him earlier, who crumbled in the aftermath of abdication and had to take to her bed.

Thus she did not see her husband proclaimed King as Wallis had seen David so proclaimed only a few short months before. But Bertie's mother had her two small granddaughters with her to witness the ceremony. Lilibet was ten now and Margaret six, both too young to have more than a hazy idea of what had happened for all that they were respectively first and second in line of succession. 'That's Mummy now,' Lilibet exclaimed when she saw a letter addressed to *Her Majesty The Queen* on the hall table at their Piccadilly home. She was still far from clear as to how her parents had suddenly become King and Queen. Was it something to do with Uncle David wanting to marry Mrs Baldwin? she asked her nanny.

The two girls were waiting in the hallway of 145 Piccadilly when their father returned there for the first time as King. They were there by design, not accident, and as he entered the house they both bobbed a curtsey as Gan Gan had taught them.

For the moment Bertie was taken completely aback. Emotion robbed him of words and, silently, he drew his daughters to him, embracing and kissing them both.

That evening there was a dinner party at Royal Lodge. It

was very much a family affair – the four sons of Grand-papa England, their sister and mother along with their mother's brother, the Earl of Athlone and his wife, Princess Alice. Now that it was all over, the decision irrevocably taken, no going back, David seemed more his old bright bubbling self, dominating the dinner table with his conversation. Bertie was more subdued. 'And this is the man we are losing,' he murmured at one stage.

Dinner over, David drove to Windsor Castle to make his farewell broadcast. The name by which he should be introduced to the nation now that he was King no longer had presented a problem. 'Mr Edward Windsor' had been suggested. It was a suggestion which horrified Bertie. His brother must broadcast as 'Prince Edward' he insisted.

Those left behind at Royal Lodge sat in a group, listening to his broadcast. 'To give up all this for that,' murmured his mother.

His farewell broadcast over, David returned to Royal Lodge. It was approaching midnight when his mother and sister said their goodbyes to him and left. It was 'a dark, gloomy day', his mother said. Left alone, the four brothers suddenly found themselves with nothing to say. Presently David stood up, bowed to the younger brother who was now his King and moved towards the door. Bertie followed.

'It isn't possible. It isn't happening,' George cried, despairingly.

But it was.

In the doorway the two brothers – the one who was now King and the other who was King no longer – were caught up by the emotion of the moment. They embraced and kissed each other. Then David turned quickly away, climbed into the waiting car and drove through the darkness to Portsmouth where the destroyer *Fury* was waiting to carry him out of the country. Britain could not have two Kings.

4

Family Rift

Though the two elder brothers, the new King and the old, had parted on emotional and affectionate terms, David's going was to mark the start of a family rift which lasted nearly thirty years and, even then, was not to be completely healed. Bertie had no desire to be at loggerheads with his brother and, left to his own devices, would probably have tried to patch things up. But he was no more his own master as King than David had been and too unsure of himself in his early days of monarchy to go against the advice he received from others. Within the family too, some were less forgiving of David's conduct.

Their mother, dutifully regal to her fingertips, never entirely forgave him for what she saw as his dereliction of royal duty. During the remaining sixteen years of her life she never once met the daughter-in-law for whom her eldest son had sacrificed a throne. Nor could Bertie's wife, the sister-in-law to whom David had once been so attached, bring herself to have anything more to do with either him or his American wife. She was not to meet him again until her husband's funeral, fifteen years in the future, and even then she barely spoke to him. Her personal feelings got in the way. She, more than anyone, witnessed the strain to which her husband was subject in a role thrust upon him by his brother's abdication and for which he was physically ill-equipped. She believed, and she was almost certainly right, that it shortened his life.

David's going meant another gloomy Christmas for the family, the second in a row. There was one bright spot. The birth on Christmas Day of another baby to George and Marina, a girl, Alexandra. It was, said George's mother, the first nice thing to have happened all year.

Wallis, when she fled from Britain earlier, had taken refuge in France, in the Cannes villa of Herman and Katherine Rogers, a couple she had first met in Peking in the days when she was married to Earl Winfield Spencer Jr. Though her divorce plea had been granted, there was always an outside chance that it might not yet be made absolute. The King's Proctor might yet intervene if there were grounds to suppose that there had been collusion between her and Ernest, her husband, in the matter of evidence. Or if she co-habited with David during the months of waiting. To avoid even the slightest suspicion of that, David stayed well clear of France, taking up residence at Schloss Enzesfeld, the Rothschild house near Vienna. His sister Mary and her husband, 'Lucky' Lascelles, visited him while he was there. So did the youngest of his brothers, George, and his cousin and close friend, Dickie Mountbatten. Dickie offered to be his best man when the time came to marry Wallis. David thanked him, but said No. His brothers, Harry and George, would be his supporters at the wedding, he said. That was to be only one of several disappointments which lay in store for him in the immediate future.

If they could not be with each other, he and Wallis could, and did, telephone each other daily. David also put in frequent telephone calls to Bertie, who had moved from Piccadilly to Buckingham Palace, advising him what he should and should not do now that he was King. If Bertie was not unduly put out by his brother's telephone calls, others were. Britain could not have two kings at the helm of monarchy and it was conveyed to David as diplomatically as possible that such calls must cease. Self-centred as he was, he took umbrage at this. And he was outraged by what happened shortly afterwards.

On the day Wallis' divorce was made absolute he left Vienna for the Chateau de Candé, near Tours, where they were to be married. Wallis was already there, waiting to welcome him. Then, shortly before the wedding, came the hardest blow of all, a blow David was never to forgive, and which was to make him as bitter and obstinate on his side of the family rift as his mother and at least two of his sisters-in-law were on the other. It took the form of a letter from his brother Bertie. In it Bertie broke the news which was to become a formal act of kingship on 27 May when, in a declaration made under the Great Seal of the Realm, he made David Duke of Windsor and granted him 'the title style or attribute of Royal Highness'. But this title, style or attribute, Bertie's letter went on, would not apply to David's wife nor to any children they might have.

It was not Bertie's personal wish to deprive his future sister-in-law of a rank which Harry and George's wives had held ever since marriage. It was a decision taken by the Cabinet which he had no option but to implement. Looking far into the future, those oh-so-wise statesmen wanted no possible pretenders to the throne, descendants of an ex-King, lurking across the Channel as there had been in the aftermath of James II's flight from Britain. Cabinet wisdom, however, did not extend to foretelling the future. Had it done, there would have been no need for such stringent precautions and the family rift might have been healed that much sooner. A year after marrying David, Wallis was to undergo a hysterectomy which left no possibility of ever having children. The ex-King's line would die out with his death.

It had been 'a painful action' for him to be obliged to take, Bertie said in his letter, and he hoped David would not take it 'as an insult'.

David did take it as an insult. 'A nice wedding present', he termed it. He was furious at the time and his fury was to continue to smoulder for years to come, occasionally erupting into flame. It was not only insulting, he said, but unconstitutional. He had been born a Prince. Now that he was King no longer, he was automatically a Prince again. And so the woman he married automatically became a Princess, equal to the wives of his two younger brothers, he insisted.

He and Wallis were married at the Chateau de Candé on 3 June 1937. The high hopes he had entertained earlier of making the occasion a pleasant family reunion did not mature. He had hoped his mother would be there. She wasn't, though she sent him a telegram of good wishes, as did Bertie and Elizabeth. He had hoped that Harry and George would be his supporters, as he had been one of theirs. They weren't, though they sent gifts. Nor was cousin Dickie around so that David could take him up on his earlier offer to be best man. In all the fuss and bother, no one had thought to send him an invitation. Instead, at the last moment, David had to ask his old friend 'Fruity', Major Edward Metcalfe, to be best man. Wallis was married in the name of Warfield, the maiden name to which she had reverted when her divorce from Ernest was made absolute. 'Alas! the wedding day in France of David and Mrs Warfield,' David's mother noted in her diary. And if his sister-in-law, Bertie's wife, was not to blame for the way he and his new Duchess had been treated, David certainly thought she was.

Nor was this series of family upsets yet at an end. George and Marina found themselves on holiday in Austria at the same time that David and Wallis were honeymooning there. David invited them for a visit and George wanted to accept. Marina refused pointblank. David had never been her favourite brother-in-law, as he had once been Elizabeth's, and as George's wife she had resented the influence David sometimes seemed to exercise over him. In the hope of persuading her to change her mind about visiting David, George appealed to Bertie in

55

London. Bertie saw no harm in the proposed visit. It would be quite all right, he said. Despite this, Marina still refused to go and George felt he could hardly do so without her.

Not all the members of the family were so resentful towards David. Once he and Wallis had settled in Paris, in a house in the Bois de Boulogne, there was a visit from Harry and Alice. David's abdication had had its effect on Harry too. As the next eldest brother, he had been appointed Regent to act for Lilibet in the event that anything happened to Bertie and she succeeded to the throne while still a child. It had meant sacrificing his army career and any hope of ever commanding the 10th Hussars. Even so, he bore David no animosity and was anxious to repair the family rift.

There was, it seems, some talk between them about the possibility of David returning to Britain. He wanted to return, David said, but felt he could hardly do so if Wallis was not to be accorded the same royal status as the other wives. But when Harry returned to London with news of what David had said, George was the only one who saw any validity in David's side of the argument. Of all the family, Bertie's wife, Elizabeth, was perhaps most relieved to hear what David had said. The last thing she desired was for him to return to Britain. More clearly than anyone else, she realised how much his charm and confidence might draw attention to the lack of these qualities in her husband who was now King.

As far as possible, Bertie did his best to make amends to David for the edict he regarded as so insulting. Balmoral and Sandringham do not belong to the state, as do Buckingham Palace and Windsor Castle. They are the family's private property. David had inherited them as eldest son, not King, when Grandpapa England died, and they were still his. Eager for them to remain in the family rather than be sold to some outsider, Bertie offered to buy them from him. The purchase price was substantial, believed to be in the region of £1 million, and considerably depleted his personal finances. He also arranged for David to have an allowance of £60,000 a year.

The title which Bertie had not been prepared to grant Wallis, David himself bestowed on her, however unofficially. To him, she was always Her Royal Highness and he insisted on everyone around them, friends, servants at their Paris home and people they met on their travels outside Britain, addressing her in like fashion.

Bertie too had problems. Untrained as he felt himself to be, lacking confidence, never the fittest of men, he found it no easy task to don the kingly shoes worn by his father and elder brother before him. But for his wife's help and support, he would probably – as he said himself – have found the burden too great. It was she more than anyone who made a King of him.

Under the stress of monarchy, the stammer Bertie had so painstakingly learned to control now got the better of him again and he was dreading the 'Speech from the Throne' he would have to make when he opened Parliament for the first time.

The Speech from the Throne was different from any other speech he had made. Other speeches could be drafted to avoid those words he found most difficult, but the speech from the Throne, which outlines government policy for the parliamentary year ahead, though delivered by the sovereign, is written by the prime minister. There was no way, Bertie felt, in which he could interfere.

It was his wife who saw a way out. She sent for an advance copy of the speech. She arranged for the crown Bertie would wear to be sent to the palace from its keeping place in the Tower of London. And then she sent for Lionel Logue.

In the privacy of his study, the crown on his head, his robe of state draped about his shoulders, helped by Logue, encouraged by his wife, Bertie rehearsed the speech again and again and again . . . until in the end, lengthy though it was, he knew it almost by heart. At the opening of Parliament, as when he opened that earlier Parliament in Australia, there was hardly a trace of his stammer.

Queen though she was now, Elizabeth never forgot that she was also a wife and mother. Buckingham Palace, with its hundreds of rooms, its miles of red-carpeted corridor, seemed a vast and impersonal place after the cosy intimacy of 145 Piccadilly. Lilibet, in particular, did not like it. You needed a bicycle to get round it, she said, jokingly, and, more wistfully, wished for a secret tunnel so that she might slip back to her old home to sleep at night. But her mother saw no reason why the palace, huge though it was, could not also be cosy, happy, homely. She set about making their own suite of rooms into a home within a palace. She had the rooms re-decorated in warm pastel shades. She had flowers brought in from the garden to add colour and life. She sent her favourite Scottish recipes down to the kitchen to form the basis of family meals. She had a hutch built in the garden so that the children could keep pet rabbits. She saw to it that Bertie had the right diet, the necessary relaxation and exercise. She encouraged him when he was down, calmed him when he lost his temper, as he sometimes did under the stress and strain of it all.

Queen Mary was equally concerned, but more for Lilibet than Bertie. Unless the son and daughter-in-law who were now King and Queen yet had a son, which seemed improbable with Elizabeth in her late thirties, in due course Lilibet would be Queen. It was time, her grandmother thought, to broaden her education. So each Monday afternoon she would collect her granddaughter from her palace home and take her on an educational excursion. Together, they visited such places of interest as the Tower of London and Westminster Abbey, the British Museum, the Bank of England and the Royal Mint. Bertie too was resolved that his small daughter, when her time came to don the Crown, should be better equipped for the task than he had been. So, young as she was, he began taking her with him to public functions, to Greenwich to open the National Maritime Museum, to Windsor to inspect a parade of boy scouts. She stood beside him when he welcomed President LeBrun of France on a state visit to London. He had a special picture book made for her to explain the significance of the coronation ceremony. Not to be outdone, Gan-Gan unearthed a Victorian peepshow of George IV's coronation procession from her large collection of historical bygones.

A serious, thoughtful child for the most part, only very occasionally rebellious or involved in scrapes, Lilibet absorbed it all as a sponge soaks up water. The burden of future monarchy already seemed to have settled on her young shoulders. But sometimes the child broke through the Princess and she wished herself back in the old days before Papa had been King and when he had had more free time to play with her and Margo.

She was a leggy thirteen in the summer of 1939, and Margaret, a plumpish, giggling, mischievous eight-year-old, when their father had the nostalgic notion of re-visiting the naval training college at Dartmouth where he had once been a youthful cadet. To Bertie, it was essentially a private, rather than official, occasion and he had his wife and two small daughters along for company. Also in the party, now naval ADC to the new King as he had earlier been to his elder brother, was cousin Dickie Mountbatten.

He too had been a cadet at Dartmouth as an adolescent and the two men shared many a reminiscent chuckle. Bertie had the old punishment book rooted out, turned up his own name and recalled how he had been whacked for letting off fireworks. Amidst all this nostalgic male humour, his wife was more concerned for their daughters, worried that they might pick up a virus infection which was prevalent at Dartmouth at the time.

Perhaps it would be safer if they did not attend a service arranged in the college chapel, she observed.

59

Philip could help to keep them amused, suggested Dickie Mountbatten.

Philip was Mountbatten's nephew, the son of his sister Alice, who had married Prince Andrew of Greece. They and their family had been exiled from Greece, along with other of the Greek royals in the early 1920s and had later separated. Following the split between his parents, Philip had lived a shuttlecock life in boarding schools and the homes of relatives. Much of his schooling had been paid for by his mother's other brother, his Uncle George, 2nd Marquess of Milford Haven. Since Uncle George's death the previous year, the younger brother, Uncle Dickie, had become his mentor and it was on his advice that Philip had become a cadet at Dartmouth when schooldays were over.

There was no real need for Philip to help out. The girls had their governess, Marion Crawford, with them and she could easily have looked after them. So whether Dickie Mountbatten, in suggesting that Philip join them, had any motive other than keeping his royal cousin's young daughters from becoming bored with it all, has remained a puzzle ever since. At eighteen, Philip was already a man; Lilibet a child still. Shrewd and far-seeing though Mountbatten was to prove himself in so many other directions, much as he was to urge Philip's courtship forward later, did he really see that far ahead on that July day in 1939? Possibly not. But equally possibly, his suggestion may have been a ploy to bring his nephew to the King's attention.

Whatever the answer, Philip himself, an extrovert and slightly cocky young man, was not over-thrilled at being asked to 'baby-sit' the two girls. Nevertheless, he put himself out to entertain them, though there was not much at Dartmouth to divert girls of any age, let alone two so young. Apart from the actual cadets, of course. If Margaret was still too young to feel the biological attraction of the opposite sex, Lilibet was not.

From the moment she saw Philip, she could scarcely take her eyes from him. Fascinated by his Viking good looks (Greece had originally imported its Royal Family from Denmark), she saw everything he did, whether operating a toy train for her amusement while it rained or playing croquet with her when the rain stopped, as beyond compare. 'How clever he is,' she murmured to her governess. She was attentive beyond the bounds of mere politeness when he stayed with them, on the second day, for afternoon tea aboard the royal yacht. 'What would you like?' she kept asking him. While the younger Margaret stared wide-eyed at the vast quantities of shrimps he was putting away, Lilibet was concerned to ensure that he had plenty of everything, blushing happily as she did so. At thirteen, she was experiencing the first pangs of puppy love.

5

Family At War

From the moment of that first meeting with Philip, the future Elizabeth II was never to love any other man. Except for her father. And him she loved in a different fashion.

From Dartmouth the family went on to Balmoral for the usual long summer vacation. But, for the parents at least, shorter than usual that year of 1939. As the war clouds darkened over Europe, Bertie felt the need to be back in London, at the heart of things. Elizabeth went with him, leaving their two daughters at Birkhall, a house on the Balmoral estate, with their governess. War or no war, they were all together again at Sandringham for Christmas.

With the outbreak of war, Dickie Mountbatten, granted command of the destroyer *Kelly*, was despatched across the Channel to bring David and his American-born wife safely back to Britain. For the two cousins who had once been so close, it was an affectionate and exciting reunion. Others in the family were less delighted by this enforced turn of events. There was talk of making David regional commissioner of Wales, a job he would have liked, but some of Bertie's advisers thought it unwise to have two kings in the country, especially when the one who was King no longer had once been Prince of Wales. His sister-in-law, Elizabeth, if she had no actual say in the final decision, was relieved when, with no sign yet of the *blitzkrieg* to come, he returned to France as a member of the British Military Mission.

Harry, the only professional soldier in the family, also went over to France, serving as Chief Liaison Officer with the British Expeditionary Force, a role which made him technically senior to David for all that the two brothers each held the rank of major-general. 'Road-hog,' David greeted him when they met on the British sector of the Belgian front, a joking reference to a long-ago motor race in Windsor Great Park between Harry in his Sunbeam and David in a Rolls Royce borrowed from their Aunt Victoria.

At Lord Gort's headquarters the 2nd Coldstreams mounted a guard of honour. When they presented arms, David took the salute. Always a stickler for protocol, so like their dead father in so many ways, Harry considered this a breach of military etiquette. David should have held back and allowed Lord Gort to take the salute as commander-in-chief, he told his brother later.

David and Wallis were still in France when the Germans overran the country, retreating ahead of the advancing enemy to Biarritz where they had once holidayed together and friendship had turned to love. They managed to cross into Spain and from there made their way to Portugal, to Lisbon. Winston Churchill, who had taken over as Britain's war-time prime minister, sent a flying boat to bring them back to Britain. But David dug his heels in and refused to come. He had been 'bloody shabbily treated', he said, and would return to Britain only if Wallis was given the same royal status as the wives of Harry and George.

While there was now no question of David and Wallis having children, there was still the possibility –or so some thought – that Wallis, already twice divorced, might yet divorce her third husband. In that far less permissive age the spectre of the King's ex-King brother being involved in a divorce action was a horrifying one. And suppose a divorced Wallis should marry for a fourth time? She would still be Her Royal Highness, whatever her fourth husband, for the title, once given, could not then be taken away. Or suppose a divorced David should decide to marry again. Would he then insist on his second wife also being accorded the title of Royal Highness? Bertie was advised that he must not give in to his brother. Instead of returning to Britain, David was offered an appointment as Governor of the Bahamas. The offer was an insult to someone of his status, he said. But he accepted it just the same.

Bertie could have well done without this further bickering with the brother from whom he had taken over. War itself was a sufficient strain on him. But war also brought out his true strength of character. If Winston Churchill was the rock upon which victory over Germany was finally to be forged, then Bertie and his devoted, supportive wife were an inspiration when things looked blackest.

With a large part of London laid waste by German aerial bombardment, Bertie insisted on continuing to use Buckingham Palace as his daytime headquarters, his royal standard flying defiantly from its masthead. At night they slept at Royal Lodge with the girls nearby in the greater security of Windsor Castle. They returned together one morning to find many of the palace windows shattered. A few days later they were there when the palace was again bombed. Through a window they actually saw the bombs falling. Bertie pulled Elizabeth down under a table for safety as a stick of six bombs exploded in line from the forecourt at the front of the palace to the gardens at the back, wrecking the chapel in the process. 'We all wondered why we weren't dead,' Bertie noted in his diary.

Despite the narrowness of their escape, he continued to work at the palace. And a suggestion that they should move to a room with smaller windows which could be boarded over against the possibility of further bombs was vetoed by Elizabeth. 'We must be able to see the sunshine,' she said. Similarly, she rejected the idea of sending their daughters to safety in Canada.

The girls remained instead at Windsor. At night they could hear the bombs crumping down on London. When the air-raid siren went they took refuge in the castle basement.

The first time this happened there was some delay in getting them downstairs from their bedroom to the basement. The modest, serious Lilibet was to blame. She flatly refused to be seen in her nightwear and insisted on fully dressing herself. To speed things up on subsequent occasions, one-piece 'siren suits' were made which she and Margaret could slip on over their nightdresses.

The two girls took part in fire drill and anti-gas drill, helped to collect scrap metal for aircraft production, and knitted 'comforts' for relatives and servants who were now in the armed forces. Those same relatives and servants also received letters of encouragement from Lilibet written in a round schoolgirl hand (though she had never actually been to school). Among those she wrote to was Philip and she also sent him a pair of socks she had knitted. The socks were somewhat shapeless – she was never particularly good at knitting – but Philip sent her a letter of thanks from Durban. He was now in the Navy and had already been in action aboard the battleship *Valiant* at the battle of Cape Matapan. Lilibet was thrilled with his letter and the following year, when he arrived back in Britain with a spot of leave due to him, she persuaded her parents to invite him to tea at Royal Lodge.

With Elizabeth, Bertie toured bomb-shattered London, picking their way through the still smoking ruins, as well as visiting other devastated cities up and down the country. Not content with this, he had lathes installed so that he and his aides could do their own spot of production towards Britain's war effort and, following the downfall of France, with every indication that Britain was next in line for invasion, he took a firearms course, learning to handle both a pistol and a sten gun. Elizabeth also learned to handle firearms. Tirelessly, as the war ran its course, Bertie visited shipyards and factories, the Home Fleet, RAF stations and US bases, the battlefronts in France, North Africa, Malta. Worried though she was for him when he went overseas, Elizabeth encouraged him to go. He insisted on personally presenting awards for gallantry to all ranks and not merely to officers, as had previously been the royal custom. He devised the George Cross and the George Medal as matching awards for civilians and they were based on a design he roughed out personally. It was his own idea too to give the Victoria Cross posthumously to Captain Fogarty Fegen of the *Jervis Bay* when he sacrificed both his ship and his own life to protect an Atlantic convoy from the German pocket battleship *Admiral Scheer*.

Queen Mary spent most of the war years at Badminton with her niece, the Duchess of Beaufort. Travelling there in convoy with practically the whole of her Marlborough House staff, plus their wives and children, hindsight gives a curiously coincidental twist to the fact that she should have stopped for lunch at Althorp Hall with Lord and Lady Spencer whose unborn granddaughter, years in the future, would marry Bertie's grandson and become Princess of Wales.

Gan Gan was seventy-two when war broke out, but as indefatigable as ever. 'I feel useless here', she wrote from Badminton. She drove around in her high-bodied Daimler, visiting hospitals, factories, evacuated families, stopping the car to give lifts to hitch-hiking Servicemen. She bought shirts and socks for troops snatched from the Dunkirk beaches. She organised evacuee children into a salvage team and went round with them collecting any old bottles, tin and scrap iron she could find. Indeed, she was sometimes a shade too enthusiastic and members of her staff surreptitiously had to return harrows and similar agricultural implements to irate farmers.

Others of the family also played their part in the war effort. Bertie's sister Mary served as head of the Red

Cross, the RAF Nursing Service and the Auxiliary Territorial Service. Her two sons, George and Gerald, both served with the Grenadiers and George was later, towards the end of the war, to be taken prisoner during the Allied offensive in Italy.

Harry was wounded at Tournai when a shell from a German dive-bomber blasted his car. He bled profusely, but fortunately the wound proved not too serious. Following Dunkirk, however, it was deemed wiser that his army duties should be mainly confined to Britain. Not to keep him out of harm's way, but so that he would stay in one piece to act as Regent to Lilibet in the event that Bertie did not get back safely from one of his visits to the war zones. From Britain, Harry too did his share of visiting the various war zones – Gibraltar, the Western Desert, hotspots in the Middle East and India. His wife, the quiet, self-effacing Alice, became head of the Woman's Auxiliary Air Force.

Their marriage had so far proved childless. There had been one pregnancy, but it had ended in a miscarriage. Others in the family murmured that Alice's fondness for riding and hunting was perhaps to blame. Then in 1941 she again found herself pregnant. In the light of what had happened before, she decided to enter a nursing home where a son, William, was born by Caesarian section two weeks before her fortieth birthday.

George and Marina should have gone to Australia in 1939, where George would have been Governor General. Arrangements for the trip were already complete, staff appointed, furnishings for Government House selected and their horses shipped out ahead of them, when war intervened. Instead of going to Australia, George went into the Air Force and was appointed to the staff of the Inspector General with the rank of group captain. Marina became commandant-in-chief of the Women's Royal Naval Service. Under the pseudonym of 'Nurse Kay' (K for Kent), she also worked as an auxiliary nurse at

University College Hospital in London, making beds and tea, serving meals, washing patients and changing dressings. Few others in the hospital knew that her husband was both the King's brother and the hospital president. To keep up her harmless deceit, Marina even curtsied to him the day he popped into her ward during a visit of inspection.

As a group captain on the Inspector General's staff George was kept busy visiting RAF stations both in Britain and overseas. He flew out to Canada to see how the Commonwealth Air Training Plan was coming along and went on to the United States to visit aircraft factories and cement goodwill relations with President Roosevelt. The two men quickly became friends and when Marina gave birth to her third child, another boy, in 1942, they added a fourth name of Franklin to his first name of Michael in honour of the American president. They also invited him to be one of the baby's godparents and he readily accepted. Baby Michael was only seven weeks old when George kissed Marina goodbye yet again and set off to visit British troops based in Iceland.

His flying boat took off from the Cromarty Firth on the afternoon of 25 August 1942. It was a calm, windless day with the sea as smooth as a tablet of grey slate. Aboard the Sunderland, in addition to George, were his secretary, his equerry, a batman and a crew of ten, as well as the commanding officer of the squadron who had come along to ensure that their VIP passenger was well looked after. The flying boat skimmed a few feet above the water to the mouth of the estuary, where it climbed to something between 1000 and 1500 feet and headed north for Iceland, following the coastline at a steady 115–120 knots. They had been airborne for less than half an hour when they ran into heavy cloud.

The cloud blotted out all sight of the coastline below. The flying boat descended slightly for the pilot to pick up his markers again. Descending, it drifted inland, flew into a hillside and exploded.

Of the fifteen men on board, only the tail-gunner, Andrew

Jack, survived the crash. Regaining consciousness, he staggered around, his face and arms badly burned, one hand broken. The remnants of the engines still smouldered in the heather. He recognised George's body by the insignia of rank on the sleeve and the gold-inlaid articles from his dressing case which were scattered around it.

In pain and barely conscious of what he was doing, driven on by the instinct for survival, he stumbled along a meandering path by the side of a stream. Darkness came soon afterwards and he slept, exhausted, on a bed of fern. With the coming of dawn he was still so exhausted he could walk barely two hundred yards at a time. Eventually he came upon a small cottage and collapsed on the grass patch which fronted it. By that time others had already located the crashed aircraft.

It was late at night when news of George's death was telephoned to Coppins, the country home where he had said goodbye to Marina for the last time. She was in bed. The butler took the call and broke the news to Kate Fox, who had been Marina's nanny in childhood and had come out of retirement to help look after the new baby. And it fell to Kate Fox to tell Marina the tragic news.

Bertie and Elizabeth were at Balmoral when news of George's death was received. Harry and Alice were staying with them. Harry, in particular, was hard hit by his brother's death. 'A nightmare', he termed it. Bertie motored from Balmoral to view the scene of the disaster. 'I felt I had to do this pilgrimage', he noted in his diary. He also arranged for Marina's sister Olga to fly from South Africa to comfort her sister in her loss of a husband, not yet forty.

For days Marina was prostrate with grief. For weeks she hardly left the environs of Coppins. Work became the eventual antidote. She took on more and more, George's work as well as her own. For instance, she took over the presidency of the RAF Benevolent Fund which he had held. Later, when she felt up to it, she went to see the spot where he had died. She journeyed to Scotland and had one of the locals guide her across the moors to Eagle's Rock, the scene of the crash, where she sat for a long time amidst the heather, alone with her thoughts. Later still, when the children were of an age to understand, she was to make one more pilgrimage to Eagle's Rock, taking them with her.

Of all the family, immediate and extended, perhaps it was cousin Dickie who was to find his true vocation in war. Saved from a watery Mediterranean grave when his destroyer, the almost legendary *Kelly*, was sunk under him with the loss of 130 lives, he went on to become head of Combined Operations, responsible for much of the preliminary groundwork for D-Day, and allied 'Supremo' in South-East Asia where he had already turned the tide of war against Japan even before the atom bomb attack on Hiroshima. War also brought a new relationship into his marriage when Edwina joined him in South-East Asia, her tremendous vitality now finding a worthwhile outlet in work for refugees and the wounded. In her forties, she was as indefatigable as ever and the collapse of Japan found her busily organising the repatriation of internees and prisoners of war. As impulsive and unpredictable as ever too, reaching Sumatra ahead of even the liberating troops.

At Windsor, during the war years, Lilibet grew up. She was a child of thirteen when war broke out; a young woman of nineteen when it ended. As girlhood merged almost imperceptibly into young womanhood, she experimented with lipstick, so amateurishly at first that her lips looked as though they were smeared with raspberry jam. She wrote more letters to Philip. With one of them she enclosed a photograph of herself, signed 'Lilibet'. He sent her one of himself in return. In 1943, when he was again on leave in Britain, she persuaded her parents to invite him for Christmas.

That was the Christmas she starred as principal boy in

70

an amateur version of the pantomime *Aladdin*. She was sixteen, approaching seventeen, and appeared on stage in a short, close-fitting tunic and glistening silk tights which showed her legs off to perfection. Philip was in the audience, sitting between Lilibet's parents, and something Bertie sensed that night gave him reason for thought. Later, when Philip was not around, he dropped a teasing remark about him into conversation with his elder daughter and was intrigued to see her blush beetroot-red.

That she was attracted to Philip became increasingly obvious. She could no more keep him out of her speech than out of her thoughts. Whatever the subject of conversation, she would find a way to bring Philip into it. It was always 'Philip this' or 'Philip that'. Even so, Bertie was rather taken aback when he met Philip's cousin, George II of Greece, at the wartime marriage of King Peter of Yugoslavia, and the Greek took advantage of the occasion to raise the question of Philip and Lilibet marrying.

He liked Philip, Bertie said, collecting his thoughts. 'He is intelligent, has a good sense of humour and thinks about things the right way. But Lilibet is too young for that now. Besides, she has never met any other young men of her own age.' Philip, he concluded, 'had better not think any more about it for the present.'

Lilibet was constantly badgering her father to be permitted to do what she called 'some proper war work'. Bertie demurred. She was heir to his throne and training for future monarchy, he felt, was job enough. There was always the risk that he would be killed in a crash, as his youngest brother had been, or be shot down on a flying visit to one of the battlefronts. At any time, at a moment's notice, Lilibet might find herself Queen. If that time should come, he wanted her to be better equipped for the task than he had been himself when his brother abdicated. To this end, he intensified her training, going through the contents of his 'boxes' with her, showing her the secret papers which reached him daily from the prime minister and others.

They were, as she grew into young womanhood, more than merely father and daughter, monarch and heir. They were good friends too in a close-knit, warmly affectionate relationship. She shared not only his sense of royal duty, but his fondness for Sandringham, his enthusiasm for horse racing, among other things.

Bertie loved his younger daughter too, but in different fashion. She was the fun child of the family. She made him laugh, he said. But she was not his heir, as Lilibet was. Between him and Lilibet there was a special, almost mystical, bond which did not exist with Margaret.

With the approach of Lilibet's eighteenth birthday, he urged Parliament that she was of an age to serve as a Counsellor of State. Counsellors of State are the monarch's deputies, selected members of the family who can act on behalf of the monarch if he/she is ill or absent from the country. Until then, no one under the age of twenty-one had been considered sufficiently mature to carry out this function. But, said Bertie, he wanted his elder daughter to have every opportunity of gaining experience 'in the duties which would fall upon her in the event of her acceding to the throne'. Aware of the risks to which he was constantly exposed on trips to the various war zones, Parliament took his point and agreed to the change.

That was shortly before the D-Day landings in Europe, with very considerable risk for Bertie if he went ahead with his notion that, as King, he should sail personally with the invasion fleet.

He got that idea from his prime minister, Winston Churchill. Old war-horse that he was, Churchill revealed to Bertie that he proposed to be where the action was on D-Day. The idea had an heroic ring to it which appealed strongly to Bertie's sense of history and destiny. If the prime minister could go, he thought, then why not the commander-in-chief? Why should a King not once again lead his troops into battle or if not into actual battle, at least be there to encourage and cheer them on as they landed in Hitler's fortress Europe?

He discussed the idea with his wife. Close as they were, inseparable as they nearly always were, they worried for each other whenever royal duty obliged them to be apart. Elizabeth had been particularly worried for Bertie in 1943 when he flew to congratulate troops in North Africa on their desert victory. On that occasion, his aircraft should have made a refuelling stop at Gibraltar, but Gibraltar was shrouded in fog and they had to fly on. Elizabeth, back in Britain, had expected to hear that her husband had landed at Gibraltar around eight o'clock that night. As the hours ticked by without word, 'I imagined every sort of horror, and walked up and down my room staring at the telephone,' she told Bertie's mother in a letter. Word that her husband was safe finally reached her only after his aircraft had touched down in Africa.

If Bertie went through with his idea of sailing with the invasion fleet, she knew she would worry again. Yet she encouraged him to go. 'He feels so much not being more in the fighting line,' she confided in her mother-in-law.

But if she was willing for him to go, others were horrified at the whole idea. It was a hare-brained scheme, far too risky, they murmured among themselves. What if the King and Churchill were both killed? Neither of them should go. But how in the world to dissuade them?

It was the King's private secretary, Sir Alan Lascelles, who finally found a way out. Tongue in cheek, he put a shrewd question to the King. In the event that neither King nor prime minister survived their D-Day sortie, what advice should he himself tender the new, young Queen concerning her appointment of a new prime minister?

Bertie took his point and changed his mind about going. There remained the question of how to prevent Churchill, so often a law unto himself, from sailing with the invasion fleet as originally planned.

Taking a leaf out of his private secretary's book, Bertie devised a form of words he hoped would do the trick. If he, as King and head of the armed forces, could not sail with the invasion fleet, he wrote to Churchill, by what right did his prime minister propose to do so?

The King's note, diplomatically phrased though it was, was still tantamount to a royal command. In consequence, when the invasion fleet sailed for the beaches of Europe, prime minister, as well as monarch, remained safely in Britain.

With Lilibet now of an age when, in the event of her father's death, she could succeed to the throne without the necessity for a Regent, there was no longer need for her Uncle Harry to stay in Britain. Australia still required a member of the Royal Family as Governor-General. There could be no question of giving the job to David, of course, and with George, who should have gone there, now dead, only Harry remained available. The war was not yet over when he and Alice with their two sons – the second, Richard, had been born, also by Caesarian section, when Alice was forty-three – set sail aboard the SS *Rimutaka*. Their convoy was attacked by U-boats off Ireland, but made it to safety and even succeeded in sinking one of the attackers.

Harry's tour of duty as Governor-General of Australia was not perhaps an unqualified success. With the war still very much on in the Far East, conscientiously dutiful as always, he visited Australian troops in New Guinea, New Britain and Bougainville, with a further projected trip to the war zone halted only by news of the Japanese surrender. But his shyness often made others shy and his meticulous insistence on the niceties of protocol did not always go down well with some of the down-to-earth Aussies with whom he had to rub shoulders.

Back home, Lilibet continued to harangue her father to let her do a proper job of war work. 'If others can do it, why do I have to stick around doing nothing?' she argued with him on one occasion. 'Look at Mary.' Mary was her cousin, Lady Mary Cambridge, who had trained as a nurse.

As her father pointed out, she was not 'doing nothing'. On the contrary, she was constantly busy. As Counsellor of State, she served as his deputy, signing state papers when he took off for Italy to visit Allied troops there. She dined with the Commonwealth prime ministers when they gathered in London. She launched the latest battleship, *Vanguard*, and gave the name *Rose of York* to a new Flying Fortress which, sadly, was shot down soon after during a raid on Berlin. She visited factories, mines and military establishments and, in conditions of the strictest secrecy, watched a rehearsal by the airborne forces for their part in the assault on Hitler's fortress Europe.

But all this was pretty tame stuff, compared with what Philip was doing, she felt. She wanted to do something which would make a really practical contribution to the war effort, however small. In the end her father gave way and permitted her to join the Auxiliary Territorial Service, though still insisting that she should return to Windsor each night to sleep in her own bed. As a subaltern at nearby Camberley, she learned to drive a car (and heavy vehicles), change a wheel, adjust a carburettor, dismantle and reassemble an engine. Her army experience, brief and cushioned though it was, also gave her a fleeting glimpse of life on the other side of the royal curtain. That happened the day she found herself on the receiving end of a royal inspection. The royal visitor was her Aunt Mary, Princess Royal and commandant of the ATS.

'You've no idea what a business it's been,' Lilibet sighed to her parents when she got back to Windsor again. 'Spit and polish all day long.'

6

Lilibet In Love

Dickie Mountbatten's nephew, Philip, became an increasingly frequent caller at Buckingham Palace in the utility, austerity, rationing years which followed World War II. It was an era when nearly everyone had to queue for nearly everything, when coupons as well as money were the price people paid for meat, bacon, butter, clothes, petrol, coal and other things besides. Television was still in its infancy, small screen, single channel, black and white only, but colourful, boisterous American musicals were invading the London stage. Philip took Lilibet to see one of them, *Oklahoma!* and one of its hit tunes, 'People Will Say We're In Love' became *their* song. Girls everywhere lusted after the new nylon stockings and those who couldn't get them drew imitation seams down the backs of their legs with eyebrow pencils. Lilibet was luckier than most. Visiting a hosiery factory with Gan Gan, she was given a pair. She was delighted with their sheerness, but Gan Gan was doubtful about their warmth.

'They look as though they might be rather cold to wear,' she said, holding them up to the light.

But even a princess could not have a pair of gift stockings without surrendering coupons. Lilibet promised to send the necessary three coupons as soon as she got back to Buckingham Palace. However, a woman factory worker generously offered to sacrifice three of her own precious coupons.

The years of war had turned Philip from a callow, rather cocky youth into a handsome and justifiably self-assured young naval officer, and Lilibet was more in love with him than ever. At weekends, when Bertie, Elizabeth and their two daughters adjourned to Royal Lodge, Philip would turn up there too. The wartime era of whirlwind love affairs to which some of his shipmates had succumbed had given way to a period when courtship was slow and romantic. Even so, for a variety of reasons, Philip's wooing of Lilibet was to be more drawn out than most. And perhaps less romantic than many. There were always too many other people around – her parents, her chatterbox of a sister, royal aides and servants – for romance to blossom very freely. They could seldom so much as go out for a walk without Margaret tagging along. She was there too when they sat together of an evening in Lilibet's old childhood nursery at the palace, now a cosy sitting room. Sometimes, to get away from Margaret and the rest, Philip would suggest a drive in his two-seater, a nippy little MG. A call on the widowed Marina, Philip's cousin by birth and Lilibet's aunt by marriage, afforded a reasonable excuse for an outing, and Marina had sufficient understanding of their predicament to permit them a small degree of privacy impossible to find elsewhere.

For Marina the immediate postwar years were far from easy. War had robbed her not only of a husband she loved deeply, but also of the state allowance on which the family had previously lived. The state made no provision for his widow, and the bulk of George's private fortune, amounting to a little over £150,000, had been left in trust for the elder son who had so tragically become Duke of Kent at the tender age of six. Marina could have drawn a widow's pension from the RAF – £398 a year for the widow of an air commodore at that time – but declined to do so. She would not 'humiliate' herself, she said. Instead, she sold

77

the lease of the town house in Belgrave Square and disposed of its contents and she rented out some of the land around Coppins. On what she raised in this fashion, she set about bringing up her three children in a style befitting their titles of princes and princess and did her best to maintain her own standards as Duchess of Kent with all the extra expense that that involved. There was the cost of travelling to the public functions she was expected to attend, of dressing in style, of giving generously to charity. Her early upbringing as an exiled and impoverished princess in Paris, where she had made her own dresses and hats and fixed her own hair, stood her in good stead. She came to an unofficial arrangement with some of the big London stores in the matter of clothes. An evening gown would be delivered to her 'on approval'. She would wear it at a public function and return it next day. The word-of-mouth publicity that the elegant Marina was wearing their clothes was considered a sufficient return by the stores involved.

As in less regal families, other family members rallied round in her time of need. Her mother-in-law, Queen Mary, helped out. Her brother-in-law, Lilibet's father, contributed towards the cost of the children's schooling and, later, a grace-and-favour apartment was made available at Kensington Palace to replace the house in Belgrave Square. Even so, she was obliged to cut costs in many directions. No longer could she entertain as lavishly as she had done when her husband was alive. She had to pay off some of her staff and cut down on trips abroad to see her sisters and other relatives. To keep things going, a number of family heirlooms – silver, pictures, furniture and other antiques – were sent for sale in London auction rooms from time to time. The two elder children, Eddy and Alex, initially went to a small private school nearby so that there were no boarding or travel expenses. They journeyed to and fro on bicycles and their pocket money was limited to sixpence a week. At holiday times, she took them to stay at small seaside hotels, booking in as 'Marina Kent'. It was only later, when judicious string-pulling resulted in the annual Civil List payment to the monarchy being increased by exactly the amount her husband had drawn in his lifetime, that the situation improved and she could afford to give the children the sort of education she felt necessary. She sent Alex to Heathfield, a fashionable boarding school for girls, and the two boys in turn to Eton.

There were problems too which had nothing to do with finance. Her elder son, Eddy, had adored his father and that wartime tragedy affected him deeply. Lacking a father's love, guidance and discipline, he was inclined to be a bit wild as he grew into his teens and towards manhood. It was cousin Philip who eventually suggested a cure. Just as a talk with Uncle Dickie had resulted in Philip going into the Navy, so, later, he had a talk with young Eddy along the same lines. For Eddy, it was to be the Army which provided what was needed.

Anxious not to spark off a welter of public speculation, Lilibet and Philip seldom ventured out together in a fashion which might draw attention to themselves. On the rare special occasions when they did go out dancing and dining or to a theatre it was always as two of a group. One such special outing was a theatre visit to celebrate Lilibet's twentieth birthday in 1946. There were three couples in the group that evening, with Margaret, now fifteen, as the odd one out. To make up the number, one of their father's equerries was invited to join the party. His name was Peter Townsend.

Just as it had been Bertie's idea to inaugurate the George Cross – and later to award it to what he termed 'the island fortress of Malta' – so it had been another of his wartime notions to surround himself with young men who had distinguished themselves in battle. It was in this capacity, a young group captain who had downed eleven enemy aircraft and had a toe shot off in the process, that Townsend, at the age of thirty, first appeared in the corridors of Buckingham Palace in February 1944. Margaret was then thirteen, the impressionable age at which Lilibet had first clapped eyes on Philip. Since even the more serious Lilibet had been a keen fan of such folk-heroes as Guy Gibson and Stanford Tuck during the early days of war, the effect of Townsend's actual physical presence, handsome and heroic, on the more volatile Margaret can easily be imagined. If not in love with him, as Lilibet had been from that first meeting with Philip, Margaret completely hero-worshipped him.

If her parents were aware of this, it gave them no cause for concern. To Townsend, she was initially no more than a child, one of the King's daughters. His personal life revolved around his wartime bride and their two small sons, now living in a grace-and-favour cottage at Windsor which Bertie had made available to them. He would dash home to see them at every opportunity. His duties as a royal equerry would keep him at the King's side often until midnight or even later. Full of vitality as he was, he thought nothing of snatching only a few hours of sleep, waking in time to be up, dressed and out of the palace at five in the morning, catching the first train out to Windsor to have breakfast with his wife and sons, then dashing off again to be back at the palace in time for duty at nine a.m. There were some weekends when he was technically on duty, but, because Bertie had gone to Royal Lodge, found himself with nothing to do. Those weekends, too, he would sometimes slip away to be with his family. One weekend, however, he was caught out. He was back on duty on the Monday when he let slip a remark about how splendid the weather had been at Windsor the previous days.

'How do you know?' Bertie demanded, gruffly. 'You're supposed to have been here, not there.'

But he was not really angry and Townsend knew it. There were other occasions when Bertie knew more about Townsend's comings and going than the equerry realised, but said nothing. The King increasingly treated him as a personal friend. Bertie's temper had never been of the best and the strain of wartime monarchy made him even quicker to flare (though he was always sorry afterwards). The older hands among royal aides, aware of the strain on him, made allowances for his outbursts. Newcomers like Townsend could not be expected to understand and, for this reason, were usually rotated at intervals of a few months. But while other of these young temporary aides came and went, Townsend stayed on and on and on. Bertie liked the man.

He liked Philip too, who seemed to be always around these days. That Lilibet and Philip thought themselves in love was increasingly becoming clear to him, but he was concerned as to whether Lilibet was sufficiently mature to know her own mind. Her upbringing, he realised, had been extremely cloistered and wartime security at Windsor, when she was in her teens, had made it even more so. As he remarked to his wife, what other young men had she ever had the opportunity of meeting and getting to know? Precious few.

He set about doing something to remedy that situation. Other young men, eligible bachelors of suitable background, were invited to Windsor for the Royal Ascot house party, to Balmoral for the shooting season, to Sandringham in winter. But while Lilibet was polite and friendly to them, her heart, as she made clear to her father, was set on Philip. But likeable though Philip was in so many ways, was he the right man? Bertie was concerned both for his daughter's personal happiness and the high position she would one day occupy. As he told a close friend: 'One day Lilibet will be Queen. Philip will be her Consort. And that's the hardest job in the world. Far harder than being King.'

Did Philip have the necessary qualities which would make him both a good husband and a good Consort? Bertie set about finding out. He had Philip to stay with the family at Balmoral and Sandringham. The two of them went out shooting together, tramping the Scottish moors, walking through the fields and woods of Norfolk. Just as he knew more about Townsend than the equerry realised, so Bertie quickly discovered more about his future son-in-law than Philip may have realised.

Bertie found himself warming to the young man. He might be no great shakes with a gun, but he was determined to learn. Bertie admired determination in a man. He liked his confidence too, even if it was sometimes misplaced. And his blunt naval way of expressing himself and his belly-laugh sense of humour. For his part, Philip was a lot less confident than he appeared the first time he stayed at Balmoral. There was a degree of awe, something which always remained, in his attitude to Lilibet's gruffly-spoken and sometimes irascible father. He was conscious of the paucity of his wardrobe. He had gone almost straight from school into the wartime Navy and, apart from uniforms, there had been little time to bother with clothes. And not much money to do anything about it since. He had no kilt, of course. Why should he? He was in the Navy, not the Scots Guards. Bertie lent him one. It was the wrong length and everyone laughed when he appeared in it, Philip included. His evening jacket was borrowed from Uncle Dickie. His walking-out shoes soon disintegrated under the wiry impact of Scottish heather and he was forced to take a day's breather while they were repaired. None of which really mattered. What mattered was that Bertie came to the conclusion that Philip was 'the right man for the job', the job being that of Lilibet's future Consort.

There was another slightly less welcome visitor to the palace, if not Balmoral, in those immediate postwar years. Fed up with his post as Governor of the Bahamas, which he had always considered beneath him, David had quit unexpectedly with five months of his term of office still to go and returned to live in France. From there, despite his vow that he would not return to Britain unless and until his wife was given the status of Royal Highness, he visited his brother in London from time to time.

Wallis did not accompany him on these visits. Which was perhaps as well. His mother would not have received her – and David knew this. Eighteen months after his abdication she had written him a letter in which she made her feelings abundantly plain. 'I do not think you have ever realised the shock which the attitude you took up caused your whole family and the Nation . . . My feelings for you as your Mother remain the same, and our being parted and the cause of it grieve me beyond words. After all, all my life I have put my Country before everything else, and I simply cannot change now.'

A world war later, she still could not change. She might grieve still, but she could not forgive. Nor was his once favourite sister-in-law who was now the Queen any more forgiving. Far from receiving Wallis, she would not even see him. Whenever he visited the palace to see his brother, it seemed a curious coincidence that his sister-in-law had some engagement which meant that she had to go out just before he arrived and would not be back until he had left again. And failing a public engagement, there would be something requiring her presence at Royal Lodge and she would stay on there for tea while her husband and brother-in-law had tea together at the palace.

The main purpose of David's visits was the hope of obtaining some official appointment which would give him the status he so much desired. Contented though he was in his marriage, he missed the adulation of the old days when he had been Prince of Wales and, briefly, King. Perhaps he could serve Britain as a sort of roving ambassador, he suggested during the course of one visit. With the dread of 'two kings' still in their minds, Bertie's advisers counselled against it. And Elizabeth was perhaps not unhappy that they did. One thing could lead to another and she had no wish for her Windsor in-laws to have an excuse for returning to Britain.

Just as she had once badgered her father to be allowed to take on a proper job of war work, so Lilibet now urged him to let her and Philip be officially betrothed. Other family voices urged the same thing, some directly, others more obliquely. Marina, on the odd occasion that she met Bertie, was not above dropping a hint in favour of her cousin's suit. Dickie Mountbatten was more to the point. But still Bertie hedged. Better not to rush into things, he said.

His hesitation to give them the go-ahead was partly due to his fear of how a betrothal announcement would be received in the country. And partly it was due to his own feelings as a father.

Many fathers have a special affinity with their daughters and Bertie was no exception. But his relationship with Lilibet had grown closer and deeper than normal in recent years. They were not only father and daughter, but monarch and heir. Patiently and painstakingly he had trained her towards future monarchy as no previous monarch in history had ever trained a successor. Since she was a child of ten, when he had come unexpectedly and reluctantly to the throne, he had had her beside him on so many state and public occasions. Once she was of age, he had launched her as a princess in her own right, fixing her up with a car and a lady-in-waiting. She had sat beside him for hours as he ploughed through the contents of his boxes, explaining to her as he did so the whys and wherefores of the documents and correspondence which reached him to be studied, approved, signed. Off-duty, they had frequently gone racing together, sharing the excitement when one of Bertie's horses romped home the winner. Until now, she had always looked to him for guidance and advice. The time must inevitably come, he knew, when he must surrender her wellbeing to another and younger man, Philip. He wanted her to find the same happiness in marriage that he had found in his, but possessive of her, as both father and monarch, he was in no hurry for that day to come.

There were, in any event, plenty of difficulties to afford excuse for delay. There was the situation in Greece where monarchy still teetered on a restored throne, with Philip still technically a Greek prince. There were political complications in Britain itself. The romance between Lilibet and Philip was now the subject of newspaper speculation and, for some people, Philip had several black marks against him. Not being British was one. The fact that his four sisters were all married to Germans was another. Too many people had suffered and died in the war against Hitler to accept that with equanimity. Higher up the political scale, not all the members of the Cabinet, Foreign Secretary Ernest Bevin among them, were exactly enamoured of the idea that the heir to the throne should marry an exiled and impecunious young prince, Greek royal on one side of his family tree, Mountbatten on the other. The Beaverbrook press in particular, no admirers of Mountbatten arrogance, might be expected to foment opposition once the betrothal was announced publicly.

Philip's Uncle Dickie, now Earl Mountbatten of Burma following his wartime success as Supremo in South-East Asia, managed to get in ahead on that one. He invited the editors of the Beaverbrook newspapers round for drinks. The drinks were handed round by a tall, good-looking young man who, on that occasion, kept himself to himself. 'My nephew, Philip,' Dickie Mountbatten introduced him. He needed some advice, he said, slyly, with assumed humility, on the possibility of his Greek nephew becoming a British citizen. No mention of any marriage, but the seeds of a good press in the future had been sown.

Bertie's health, never the best, had suffered under the strain of war. He was badly run down; increasingly tetchy. But when it was suggested that a royal visit to South Africa might help that country's political stability,

85

he did not shirk. A few weeks of prolonged sunshine might do him good, he felt. In fact, it did him nothing but harm. All the travelling involved, the many functions he attended out there, served only to exhaust him further and by the time he got back he had lost seventeen pounds in weight.

He took his wife and daughters with him. Not to give Lilibet time to think, as some people assumed at the time. Her mind had long since been made up, but her father wanted them all to be together as a family and she, though she would have preferred to remain behind with Philip, wanted to please him. They could be formally betrothed immediately the trip was over, he promised her. In fact, they were unofficially betrothed even before the family left for South Africa. Accompanied by her parents, Lilibet joined Philip for a farewell dinner with Dickie and Edwina Mountbatten which turned into what was virtually an engagement party.

With Queen Mary ageing, George dead and David in exile, someone was needed to carry on the functions of monarchy while King, Queen and the heir to the throne were all absent from the country. A call went out to Harry and Alice to return from Australia. Harry had not yet completed his full term as Governor-General and, indeed, was finding it so much to his liking that he had been hoping for an extended term of office. But duty was duty. A little reluctantly, he flew home to serve as Counsellor of State during his brother's absence, leaving Alice and the boys to follow by sea.

Lilibet celebrated her twenty-first birthday while the family was in South Africa. Diamonds galore were heaped upon her to mark the occasion. Yet even more precious to her than diamonds was word from Philip that his naturalisation papers had gone through without a hitch. To the delight of Uncle Dickie, he had decided to take the name of Mountbatten, the name of his mother's family since World War I, for his future life as a British citizen.

Philippos, Prince of Greece, was now officially Lieutenant Philip Mountbatten, RN. The last obstacle to marriage with Lilibet had been removed.

If she was missing him during those weeks in South Africa, she had the excitement of marriage to anticipate. Margaret, on the other hand, dragging around at the heels of her parents, was frequently bored with it all. Their father was becoming more and more exhausted and their mother was worried about him. The task of diverting the younger daughter was delegated to the King's equerry. 'Try to keep Margaret amused, Peter.' It marked the start of a relationship between equerry and teenage princess which was to have far-reaching and unfortunate consequences.

7

The Newlyweds

Lilibet and Philip were married in Westminster Abbey on 20 November 1947. The family was there in force to wish them well. Bertie gave his daughter in marriage. Margaret was chief bridesmaid. Other bridesmaids were drawn from other sections of the extended family, Marina's ten-year-old daughter, Alex, Dickie Mountbatten's daughter, Pamela, Mary Cambridge from Queen Mary's side, Diana Bowes-Lyon, Margaret Elphinstone, Caroline Montagu-Douglas-Scott, all relatives of one sort or another. Two more youthful cousins, Harry's son, William, and Marina's son, Michael, carried the bride's train, though not without incident. Twice the train snagged on something or other and Bertie and Philip, in turn, had to help free it. To top it all, William tripped and would have fallen if Margaret had not caught him in time.

Philip had his cousin, David, 3rd Marquess of Milford Haven, as best man. More relatives – the mothers on both sides, Gan-Gan, aunts, uncles, cousins, in-laws – swelled the ranks of wedding guests. From all this vast family gathering only Bertie's eldest brother David and Philip's three sisters were missing. The sisters had not been invited. Because the bride was who she was, heir to the throne, family matters could not be divorced from affairs of state. The sisters were all married to German princes, and ex-enemies, however closely related, could hardly be invited so soon after the bloodshed of World War II.

Another family breach, as with David and his wife, could easily have resulted. It was the elegant Marina, aunt of the bride, cousin of the groom, who ensured that it did not. A few days after the wedding she flew out to Germany with a selection of wedding photographs for Philip's sisters. Unlike David at the time of his own marriage, they understood that no personal slight had been intended and all was forgiven and forgotten.

Nor did Philip take offence over the fact that his father-in-law did not restore to him the title of Prince which he had abandoned along with his Greek citizenship. Possibly it did not occur to Philip that he was not a Prince. Bertie certainly thought he had made him one when he created him Duke of Edinburgh along with the style of Royal Highness, which had been withheld from Wallis, the day before the wedding. In fact, he had not and it was left for the bride, years later, after she became Queen, to remedy her father's inadvertent omission.

Like many another girl on the threshold of marriage, Lilibet slept badly the night before the wedding. Early morning found her at the window of her bedroom, in a dressing gown, looking out at the growing crowd in front of her palace home. 'I can't believe it is really happening.' Philip, spending the night at his grandmother's Kensington Palace apartment, slept better. In fact, he overslept slightly, due to a late night: his stag party had been held the previous evening. However, a hair of the dog that bit him, in the form of a light sherry downed after breakfast, put matters to rights in good time for the actual ceremony. At Buckingham Palace, just before leaving for Westminster Abbey, Bertie similarly suggested that Lilibet should have a quick drink to steady her nerves. 'Oh, no,' she said. 'I couldn't.'

Lilibet could hardly believe, after being in love with Philip for so many years, that she was actually becoming his wife. 'I have to keep pinching myself.' Like most brides, she felt a mixture of emotions, excited by the prospect of a new life with Philip, sad at the thought of leaving her parents. Bertie too, an extremely emotional man beneath his sometimes gruff exterior, was filled with mixed emotions, 'proud and thrilled' as he escorted his daughter the length of the Abbey, but with a sense of having 'lost something very precious' at the actual moment of marriage. He took comfort from a relative's remark that he was not losing a daughter, but gaining a son. 'You're right. He belongs now.' The thought also brought a slight sense of guilt. He hoped, he wrote to his daughter a few days later, that she did not think him 'hard-hearted' for making her wait so long. She wrote back reassuring him that the long wait had probably been 'for the best'.

Bertie poured out his feelings in another letter to his now married daughter. 'Our family, us four, the "Royal Family", must remain together, with additions of course at suitable moments! I have watched you grow up all these years with pride under the skilful direction of Mummy, who as you know is the most marvellous person in the world in my eyes, and I can, I know, always count on you, and now Philip, to help us in our work. Your leaving us has left a great blank in our lives but do remember that your old home is still yours and do come back to it as much and as often as possible. I can see that you are sublimely happy with Philip, which is right but don't forget us . . .' He signed the letter: 'Your ever-loving and devoted Papa'.

Lilibet was indeed 'sublimely happy' with Philip. Under his extrovert influence, her personality, for a time, underwent a metamorphosis. She became less serious, more carefree, less regal, more feminine, sometimes even teasing and coquettish, moods which had previously been quite foreign to her nature. If he piped the tune for their married life, she was quick and happy to dance to it, giggling at his sometimes schoolboyish practical jokes, squealing in mock alarm as she fled through their borrowed apartment at Kensington Palace in her nightdress with a pyjama-clad Philip bounding athletically in pursuit.

If her marriage left a 'great blank' in her parents' lives, if Bertie in particular missed her a great deal, there was another member of the family who missed her more. Her sister, Margaret. Different though the two sisters were in temperament, Lilibet normally serious and conscientious, Margo more precocious and high-spirited, they were always close. To Margaret, Lilibet was not only her elder sister, but her dearest and closest friend. She had leaned on her all her young life, looking to her for guidance, advice, help, quietly accepting even the occasional admonition which Lilibet would dole out . . . 'Hurry up, Margaret. or we'll be late' . . . 'Copy me, Margaret, and you'll be all right.'

Now Lilibet was no longer around to advise and guide her and Margaret was thrown back on her own resources, her own judgements – and they were to prove inadequate. In some ways, she was – and is – a lot like her Uncle David, with more of Edward VII than Grandpapa England in her make-up and, lacking the steadying influence of her elder sister, this side of her nature began to emerge more and more. She grew from girlhood to womanhood as though desperate to make up for the lost childhood pleasures of the war years. Her young life became a giddy round of parties, night clubs and theatre-going. She enjoyed hob-nobbing with celebrities. She drank cocktails, took up smoking and was soon affecting a long, elegant cigarette-holder. Fun was the order of the day. A series of eligible youthful escorts danced attendance on her when she went out on the town. But within the privacy of Buckingham Palace, her earlier hero-worship of her father's equerry, Peter Townsend, was fast turning into love.

Inadvertently, her parents helped to push her into Townsend's arms. They increasingly treated him as a personal friend rather than merely a royal aide, calling him Peter, delegating him to watch over Margaret, just as he had done in South Africa. When she went to Belfast, the year her sister was married, to launch the liner *Edinburgh Castle*, Peter went with her. When she visited the Netherlands the following year for the inauguration of Queen Juliana, Peter was with her again. More and more they were thrown together and drawn together.

When the family went to Sandringham or Balmoral, Peter went with them, as much a friend as a royal aide, while in the grace-and-favour cottage at Windsor Rosemary Townsend frequently felt neglected. At Sandringham, when Philip, Bertie and the other men went out shooting, Townsend, who abhorred blood-sports, would walk and talk with Margaret. At mealtimes she would keep the chair beside her vacant until Peter showed up. If he was not yet in love with her, he no longer saw her as the child she had been when he first arrived at the palace, but as a girl of 'unusual intense beauty'. At Balmoral, while the others were again out shooting, they went riding together. Some of the hilltops around Balmoral are capped by stone cairns erected by the sentimental Queen Victoria to commemorate royal marriages and similar family occasions. One day, out riding together, Margaret and Peter conceived the idea of erecting their own personal cairn and each day after that they would race each other to the hilltop. Whichever of them reached the cairn first would add another stone. It all started as a joke, but ended as something romantically meaningful.

Margaret was excited, Bertie and Elizabeth overjoyed, when Lilibet told them that she was expecting a baby. Nothing would satisfy Bertie but that his first grandchild must be born under his own roof. Lilibet was only too willing to please him by moving back into her old home. If Philip was perhaps less delighted, he still went along with the idea uncomplainingly. Like the Prince Consort before him, he was having to adjust to the fact that a husband who marries into the Royal Family is not always the complete master in his own home. His earlier idea that he would be the bread-winner and do the paying – difficult when his wife was getting five times as much money as he was – had already taken a nasty knock. He could not, he found, afford to pay all the servants they felt were needed and Lilibet was making up the difference out of her money.

Back at the palace, they lived in their own small apartment, but ate many of their meals with Lilibet's parents. On balance, Philip got along famously with his in-laws. His mother-in-law enjoyed his practical jokes almost as much as her daughter did. If Bertie found them a bit irritating at times, he still enjoyed swapping yarns with his son-in-law about their respective naval careers.

All his life he had been plagued with poor health, knock knees in childhood, a lifelong stammer, gastric upsets in the Navy, duodenal ulcers and much else besides. Now his legs were beginning to give him trouble. He would get attacks of cramp so bad, as his brother Harry noticed when they were shooting together at Balmoral, that he had difficulty in walking. Doctors who examined him diagnosed arteriosclerosis – faulty circulation – and gave a gloomy prognosis that it might be necessary to amputate one leg. Bertie's immediate reaction was that the seriousness of his condition must be kept from Lilibet. He didn't want her upset until after she had had the baby, he said.

Something else bothered Bertie too. Lilibet was his heir. The baby, boy or girl, would be her heir, second in line of succession to the throne. Yet, as things stood, the child would be born only with one of its father's lesser titles. Just as Bertie himself had overlooked the necessity for making Philip a Prince, so Grandpapa England, in his day, had overlooked the possibility that the line of succession might one day descend through a female. He had made provision for his sons' children (though not his daughter's) to be born princes or princesses. And the children of his sons' sons. But not the children of his sons' daughters. Bertie acted to remedy his father's omission and only five days, as it turned out, before the baby's birth he authorised the title of prince or princess for the children of his elder, though not his younger, daughter. Margaret's future children were left out just as her Aunt Mary's children had been.

Lilibet, a strong, healthy girl, took her first childbirth almost in her stride. Philip, beforehand, was more worried than she was, but like a dog with two tails once he knew he had a son. Bertie was hardly less thrilled while Elizabeth, like any other grandmother, promptly began unearthing baby things hoarded sentimentally from the babyhoods of her own daughters: a pink-lined baby basket, a silver box of safety pins, a silver-backed hairbrush, a rattle and a teething ring bearing the marks of Margaret's first teeth. Relatives flocked along to see the latest chubby addition to the family circle. Great-grandmother Queen Mary brought the baby a silver gilt cup which had once belonged to its great-great-great-great-great grandfather, George III. Marina, more practically, brought along some baby clothes she had made, though enough had already flooded in from well-wishers to outfit an entire crèche of babies. Margaret, when she heard that her new nephew was to be called Charles, giggled that she would now be known as 'Charley's Aunt'.

On medical advice, Bertie continued to rest his legs as much as possible. Attempts were made to improve his faulty circulation by electric stimulation. It helped, but not enough. His plan for following up the South African tour with a similar one of Australia and New Zealand had to be called off. Instead, though amputation was avoided, a lumbar sympathectomy had to be carried out.

The operation was performed at the palace, in the same room in which the baby had been born and converted now into a temporary operating theatre. White-faced and looking deeply distressed, his wife followed as he was wheeled there on a trolley. She sat in an adjoining room, waiting for news, while the surgeons did their work and was by his bedside, ready with words of comfort and encouragement, when he came round.

Over the next few days she hardly left his side. She had her meals with him and was overjoyed when he was sufficiently recovered to revert to the rotation of scrambled egg, fried egg and omelette which he had had for breakfast every morning since they married. Once he could leave his bed, she joined him in short walks. At first, because he was not allowed to go outside, they toured the state rooms of the palace instead, taking a fresh look at the old masters and antique furnishings while their pet corgis padded patiently at their heels. Of an evening, after dinner, they sat together again just as they had done so often in their early days of marriage a quarter of a century before. No longer listening to the wireless, however, as they had done then, but watching television on a fourteen-inch screen.

A compromise between Bertie's desire to keep his daughter close to him and Philip's natural wish for a home of his own was found in Clarence House, a war-damaged royal residence not far from the palace which no member of the family had lived in since Queen Victoria's son, Arthur, moved out in 1911 to become Governor-General of Canada. Workmen set about repairing and modernising the place, with Lilibet and Philip not only popping along each day, and sometimes twice a day, to see how things were coming along, but even lending a hand with mixing paint upon occasion. When all was ready, Lilibet moved out of her parents' home and into a place of her own, happy and secure in the belief that her father was now restored to health. In fact, he was not, although it seemed so at the time. She and Philip were no longer newlyweds, but their own small family unit. Philip at last had the home of his own he had craved for so long. He settled down to being very much the family man, even to offering to lend a hand when it came to bathing baby at bedtime. With Philip around, bathtime became a rather hilarious occasion with water flying in all directions. Lilibet wisely wore a waterproof apron. Philip scorned such niceties as 'sissy stuff' and sometimes ended up with his clothing soaked.

As the King's son-in-law, Philip had been given a desk job at the Admiralty with abundant time off for indoctrination in royal chores. If none of this was unduly onerous, neither was it very satisfying to a young man with Philip's natural urge to be active. He saw no reason why, for a few years at least, he should not resume a more sea-going naval career. And back to sea he went, to HMS *Chequers*, a destroyer of the Mediterranean fleet based on Malta.

8

'Take Care Of Lilibet'

With Philip's return to the sea, Lilibet was torn between her husband and her baby. She wanted to be with both, but could hardly be in two places – Malta and Britain – at once. She could, of course, have taken the baby with her to Malta, but was worried about the change in climate. Finally, she achieved some sort of a compromise, commuting back and forth between London and Valetta as casually as other people do between, say, Peterborough and London. She first flew out to join Philip in time to celebrate their second wedding anniversary. If she wanted to stay on a few weeks longer, said her mother, then she and Grandpapa would look after baby Charles over Christmas. So Charles spent that Christmas with his grandparents at Sandringham.

'He is too sweet stumping around the room,' Lilibet's father had written her, 'and we shall love having him at Sandringham. He is the fifth generation to live there* and I hope he will get to love the place.'

Those weeks in Malta with Philip were the nearest Lilibet was ever to come to living the life of an ordinary married young woman. Even so, it was married life on a fairly exalted plane. Philip's Uncle Dickie was in Malta too

---

* Including King Edward VII in the days before the family took the name of Windsor.

at the time, commanding the First Mediterranean Cruiser Squadron, and Lilibet and Philip stayed with him and Aunt Edwina at their home on the island, the romantically named Villa Guardamangia. Lilibet loved everything about Malta, not only the scenery and the winter sunshine, but the temporary freedom from royal protocol to which, though she perhaps had not realised it until now, she had been subject from the age of ten at least. For perhaps the first time in her young life she was free to do what she wanted when she wanted, to come and go as she pleased. Well, more or less. She drove round the island in her own car, went shopping, sat with other Navy wives to have her hair shampooed and set. Polo was Uncle Dickie's favourite sport and Philip caught the bug from him. She would go along to watch him play, turning pale and springing to her feet in alarm if he took a tumble. For Christmas she bought him a polo pony. They dined and danced romantically together at a local hotel. They would take picnic lunches to deserted coves, swimming in the sea and sunning themselves on the sand. It was like a second honeymoon. Perhaps better than their real honeymoon which had been partly spoiled by the fact that Philip developed a roaring head cold. Such was their joy at being together in Malta that Lilibet, when she returned home after Christmas, found herself pregnant again.

Their second child, Anne, was born that August at the Clarence House home, a less contented, more demanding baby than Charles had been. Philip, with a spot of leave due to him, flew home to be with his wife for the baby's birth.

In the nearly three years they had been married Lilibet had done her best to make amends to her husband's sisters for the way they had been slighted at the time of their brother's wedding. While she was expecting Charles she had Philip's youngest sister, Tiny, and two of the teenage daughters of her first child-bride marriage to stay at Windlesham Moor, a country house she and Philip rented for a time near Ascot. Tiny's first marriage, like Marina's, had ended in tragedy when her husband was killed in a wartime air crash. Unlike Marina, however, she had since re-married, taking as her second husband Prince George of Hanover. Tiny had been followed as a house-guest by Dolla, the wife of Price Berthold of Baden, who also brought two of her children with her. Now, with the birth of the new baby, it was the turn of Philip's eldest sister, Margarita, wife of Prince Gottfried of Hohenlohe-Langenburg. Lilibet invited her over for the christening and asked her to be one of Anne's godparents. Even a princess can be hard up, however, and there was a small problem over the cost of the air fare. Philip generously paid it for her.

Having seen his daughter christened, Philip flew back to Malta. With another small baby to look after, it was out of the question for Lilibet to go with him. Instead, to Bertie's delight, she and the children went to stay with her parents at Balmoral. It was not quite like old times, however. Bertie still enjoyed going out shooting, but, following his operation, was obliged to do so with a long trace fastened about his waist so that a pony could help him uphill. 'What if the pony happens to bolt?' someone asked him. Grinning, Bertie demonstrated a quick-release parachute mechanism he had had fitted to the trace.

By Christmas Anne was old enough to stay with Granny and Grandpapa at Sandringham along with Charles. This left Lilibet free once again to join Philip in Malta. The Mountbattens had gone and they had the Villa Guardamangia all to themselves. Their own pictures, shipped out from London, went up on the walls, their own china and cutlery was set out on the dining table and their own porcelain ornaments adorned the niches. Unable to foresee the sudden and dramatic change in their lives which was to come in the near future, they planned to make the villa in Malta their second home for many years to come.

Philip had been promoted to the rank of lieutenant

commander and given charge of his own ship, the frigate *Magpie*. There were excursions from Malta to Italy and to Greece, where Philip showed his young wife the villa with the curiously suburban name of 'Mon Repos' in which he had been born on the dining room table. If these trips were partly in the cause of royal flag-showing, they were also personally pleasurable. Ahead of the Italian visit there was an invitation from Philip's sisters, Tiny and Dolla, to continue on into Germany and visit them at Salem, where Philip had been briefly a schoolboy in youth. But much as they would have liked to have done this, they felt obliged to turn down the invitation. It was one thing for Philip's sisters to visit them privately in Britain; quite another for his wife, the heir to the throne, to visit Germany, the old enemy.

Word that her father's health had taken a turn for the worse caused Lilibet to fly home. That June, with Bertie confined to his bed with what was said at first to be nothing more serious than a bout of influenza, she took his place at the annual ceremony of Trooping the Colour, riding side-saddle to and from Horse Guards' Parade. It was the second time she had deputised for him at the colourful and historic ceremony. On the first occasion, which followed his operation two years previously, Bertie had been able to watch from an open carriage. This time he was obliged to stay in bed and could watch the pageantry only on television.

Ill-health had earlier obliged him to cancel a planned tour of Australia and New Zealand. Now a tour of Canada, scheduled for the autumn, seemed destined to go the same route, unless Lilibet and Philip could deputise for him. Lilibet readily agreed and word was sent to Philip in Malta. Despondently, he said goodbye to the officers and crew of *Magpie*. 'It will be a long time before I want those again,' he remarked, gloomily, as his valet packed his sea-going kit. He had known all along that marriage to a King's daughter would sooner or later involve quitting the sea to take over the role of Consort, but the call had come sooner than he had envisaged.

By the time Bertie went to Balmoral for his customary summer vacation his influenza had become 'a small area of catarrhal inflammation' as far as the general public was concerned. In fact, he had cancer. He himself did not know that; was never told. He thought he had 'pneumonitis'. He told his mother, 'It is not pneumonia, but if left it might become it.' Her health too was beginning to fail. She found walking more and more difficult and sometimes had to resort to a wheelchair.

Margaret celebrated her twenty-first birthday at Balmoral that August. Peter Townsend, no longer a mere equerry but Deputy Master of the Household, bought her a sheepskin saddle as a birthday gift. Such eligible young men as Johnny, Earl of Dalkeith, and Billy Wallace were among those invited to Balmoral for the birthday celebrations, but it was Townsend, that evening, who raced up the slope which fronts the castle to light a birthday bonfire in Margaret's honour. Young and naïve as she was, she could not always conceal her feelings for him. 'Your father is watching us,' Townsend warned her the day she covered him tenderly with a coat as he dozed in the heather. Margaret merely laughed.

Bertie not only watched, but wondered. And not only wondered, but acted on the day of a family picnic. Leaving the castle, he frowned as he saw not one but two cars drawn up outside with a picnic hamper being loaded into each.

'Why two cars?' he asked.

'Margaret and Peter are going on a picnic of their own,' his wife told him.

'Oh, no, they're not,' said Bertie. 'They're coming with us.' And he gave orders for both hampers to go into one car and dismissed the second car.

Much as he doted on Margaret, fond as he was of Townsend, Bertie was not of a nature to countenance romance between his unmarried daughter and a married man. In normal circumstances, having scented danger, he would have reacted to it speedily and more forcibly. Townsend would almost certainly have been sent packing. Bertie, like his father before him, was a man of strict principles. But worry over his own health caused him to procrastinate and by the following month he was too busy fighting for his own life to be concerned any longer with what his younger daughter was doing with hers.

As his health deteriorated still further, his wife made him send for his doctors again. Examination revealed a growth in his left lung. He was told it would have to be removed, but not the reason why. Instead, he was told that a blockage of the bronchial tubes made an operation an urgent necessity. When the operation was carried out three weeks later it was discovered that his right lung was also affected. His life expectancy was, at most, two years. In fact he was to live for only a little over four months.

Worried about her father, loving him as she did, Lilibet refused to leave for Canada until after he had been operated on, successfully as she thought. By that time, with a scheduled sea crossing of the Atlantic, it was too late to get there on time. It looked as though the entire itinerary for the proposed tour would have to be hurriedly re-arranged. It was Philip who suggested, 'Why not fly there? Then we'll still make it on time.'

It was, in the early 1950s, a novel idea. Risky, prime minister Clement Attlee thought. Commuting to Malta was one thing; flying the Atlantic quite another. But Philip talked him round.

Lilibet made the trip to Canada with a heavy heart. If she did not know that her father was dying, she knew that he was far from having completely recovered. The seriousness of his condition was underlined by a special package she had to take with her. In it, in infinite detail, were full directions concerning everything she would have to do if the worst happened and she suddenly found herself Queen.

Though Lilibet did not know that her father was dying, her mother did. She faced that terrible situation with the courage and calmness she had shown all their married life, talking to him and behaving as though there was nothing wrong that would not be right again very shortly. He was, she knew, continuing to work far too hard for such a desperately sick man, perhaps shortening his life still further in the process, but she said and did nothing to deter him. His work kept him happy and that was the important thing. Nor did she or his doctors raise any objection when he wanted to smoke again. He had long been a heavy smoker, but had been persuaded to give up ahead of his operation. Now it no longer mattered much whether he smoked or not.

Lilibet telephoned daily from Canada to find out how her father was. She might smile in public, but in private she was often depressed and worried. Philip did all he could to buoy her spirits, but beneath the surface of a joking, flippant manner, he too felt the strain. Although he always went in awe of his royal father-in-law, he was fond of him too. And desperately worried for Lilibet . . .

They were home again for Christmas, spent at Sandringham as usual. It was a depressing occasion, far removed from the gaiety of earlier Christmases. Bertie was too weak even to climb the stairs and a bedroom had to be made up for him on the ground floor. When village carol singers called, as they did every year, he sat in a chair instead of standing by the piano, too tired to join in the singing. He made his customary Christmas broadcast, though not in the same way as usual. His words had been pre-recorded, a few at a time.

An apparent improvement in him cheered the others. Walking slowly through the grounds, he brought his walking stick to his shoulder like a gun. 'You know,' he said, 'I think I might shoot again.'

He did shoot again. He and Philip went out together. Bertie wore heated gloves to help the circulation in his hands and had to make use of a helping rope when the going was uphill. It exhausted him, but he thoroughly enjoyed it all.

Towards the end of January, saying goodbye to the children, Lilibet and Philip left for London. Again they were to deputise for the sick King, this time with a tour of Australia and New Zealand in place of the one he had been unable to make earlier. Ill though he was, Bertie insisted on going to London with them. As a farewell treat, he took them to see the American musical *South Pacific*. Peter Townsend was also in the party. It was the sort of belly-laugh show Bertie always preferred and he enjoyed it immensely. He insisted on going to London airport too to speed them on their way. Shortly before they boarded the aircraft he sought out 'Bobo' Mac-Donald, Lilibet's nanny in childhood and now going to Australia with her as her 'dresser'.

'Take care of Lilibet for me,' he said.

As his daughter turned to wave and smile from the doorway of the aircraft, there was a look of infinite love and sadness in his eyes. 'As though,' recalls an eye-witness, 'he sensed that he was seeing her for the last time.'

Having seen Lilibet and Philip off, Bertie returned to Sandringham – 'Dear old Sandringham' to him as it had been to his father. He found comfort in his grandchildren, having tea with them each afternoon, saying prayers with them each evening before they went to bed.

The following Tuesday, 5 February, he was again out shooting, this time with his old friend and near-neighbour, Lord Fermoy, whose unborn granddaughter would one day marry the small boy who was the King's first grandchild. It was a cold, bright winter's day, ideal for rough shooting. Bertie bagged nine hares and a wood pigeon. 'The best day's shooting I've had for a long time,' he told his friend at the end of the day. 'We'll go again on Thursday.'

He visited his grandchildren in their nursery, the first

time he had managed to climb the stairs. He sat talking to them while they had supper, said prayers with them, then went down to his own room to rest. Later, he got up again to have dinner with his wife and Margaret. After dinner he took a turn round the grounds. Indoors again, he switched on the wireless to hear the news. A little after ten he said goodnight to his wife and daughter and went to bed, taking a magazine with him.

Some time that night he died in his sleep.

His valet, James Macdonald, was the first to know. He made the discovery when he entered the room at seven o'clock the following morning with the customary pot of tea.

The wife, now widow, who had brought so much happiness into his life, who had supported him so staunchly through so many difficulties, broke down and cried when she was told. She went along to the room where Bertie's body lay and stayed there a long time. She was particularly distressed that her husband had been alone when death came.

Margaret too was grief-stricken when she learned of her father's death. She closed herself within her own room and refused to come out.

'I don't want the King left alone,' the widowed Elizabeth instructed the staff. 'Someone must stay with him, please.' Neither did she want her grandchildren's lives upset by what had happened, so she paid her customary visit to the nursery and, that evening, took her dead husband's place in saying their prayers with them. But she could not bring herself to tell them what had happened. It was the children's nanny, Helen Lightbody, who explained things to Charles as best she could. The King had 'gone away' she said when he asked where Grandpapa was.

It was some hours later before news of her father's death reached Lilibet in Kenya. It was relayed by bush telephone to the lodge near Sagana where she and Philip were staying. The call was taken by Michael Parker, Philip's longtime friend and equerry to the royal couple. He immediately went in search of Philip. 'I'm afraid there's dreadful news,' he told him. 'The King is dead.' Shock showed in Philip's face.

Lilibet was outside the lodge, enjoying a stroll in the warm sunshine. She came across Philip's valet, John Dean, cleaning a pair of shoes. Bobo MacDonald was with him. She stopped to talk to them of her plans for the following day when she and Philip were to have journeyed to Mombasa to board the liner *Gothic* for the onward trip to Australia. It had been arranged, when she and Philip returned to Britain, that her father would go to South Africa to convalesce. She wondered whether Kenya might not be better for him. 'I am sure the climate here and these peaceful surroundings would do him good,' she said.

For John Dean and Bobo, it was an awkward few moments. They already knew what she did not: that her father would never visit either South Africa or Kenya, that she and Philip would not now be going to Australia. But it was not their place to tell her. Then, to their relief, they saw Philip coming towards them. He took his wife by the arm and led her away towards the Sagana River. There, walking by the river, he broke the news of her father's death.

Presently she returned to the lodge, went to her room, closed the door behind her and cried out her grief.

By this time the solitary telephone line which linked the lodge with the outside world was in danger of becoming red hot as call after call came through from London. She emerged from her room again, looking pale and strained, to find London requiring to know what name she would take now that she was Queen.

'My own, of course – what else?'

Back to London went word that the girl her father had always called Lilibet would ascend the throne as Queen Elizabeth II.

9

Family Problems

'Take care of Lilibet', the dying Bertie had said to Bobo MacDonald when his elder daughter flew out to Kenya. 'A very tragic homecoming,' the daughter, now Queen Elizabeth II, murmured to those waiting to greet her at London airport, her own Uncle Harry and Philip's Uncle Dickie among them, in the aftermath of her father's death. The daughter might be heartbroken, but the Queen, in public, had to control her emotions. She even managed a few words to the air crew who had flown her back. 'Thank you for making me so comfortable.' Tears stayed locked behind her eyes. Winston Churchill, greeting her, let his flow openly.

At Clarence House her ageing Gan Gan was waiting to greet her. 'I wanted to be the first to kiss your hand,' she said. But her eyes were critical as she spied the black skirt her granddaughter was wearing. 'Much too short for mourning,' she commented.

Too short perhaps, but the only one available at such short notice. The mourning outfit the new Queen had taken with her (not in anticipation of her father's death, but because members of the family never travel without one) had been in one of the cases already loaded aboard the liner *Gothic*, for the onward journey to Australia and New Zealand, when the news reached her. A radio message from El Adem, where her aircraft made a refuelling stop on the homeward flight, alerted Clarence House to the problem. A substitute outfit with its 'too short' skirt was rushed to the airport and smuggled aboard the aircraft immediately it touched down. She changed out of the floral-pattern dress she had worn on the flight and into mourning as the aircraft taxied round to where her prime minister and others awaited her.

From Clarence House she telephoned her widowed mother at Sandringham. But mother and daughter could not yet share their grief in person. For the daughter, the new duties of monarchy must take precedence. Her husband and Uncle Harry accompanied her to St James's Palace, but once there she had to stand alone to take the Declaration of Accession. Again fighting back tears, she spoke of the father to whom she had been so close: 'My heart is too full for me to say more to you today than that I shall always work, as my father did throughout his reign, to uphold constitutional government and to advance the happiness and prosperity of my peoples, spread as they are the world over.'

Only when that was done was she free to leave for Sandringham. Philip drove her there.

Her father's body was already in its coffin of Sandringham oak. She was asked if she wanted to see him. She shook her head. She preferred to remember him as he was in life, she replied.

The actual funeral would be public, an occasion of national mourning for the death of a King, but behind the closed gates of their Norfolk home, his widow and daughters mourned the loss of a beloved husband and father in privacy. That night, when darkness had fallen and the moon risen, the coffin was lifted on to a wheeled bier. On top of the coffin lay a single wreath, from the elder daughter. The card was in her own handwriting: 'To darling Papa from your sorrowing Lilibet'. With her mother, sister and husband, she followed as the coffin was wheeled through the grounds, through the wrought-iron gate which separates garden from park, and across the park to the parish church.

Too frail now to attend her son's funeral, Gan Gan watched from a window as the gun-carriage bearing his body passed Marlborough House and sat in front of a television screen to view the rest of the ceremony. David came home from France for the funeral, but Wallis did not come with him. From London, the coffin was conveyed by train to Windsor, with David and his sister-in-law, brother and widow of the dead Bertie, travelling in separate railway coaches. Apart from a few conventional words of condolence and acknowledgement, they scarcely spoke to each other. If the widowed Elizabeth could not forgive her brother-in-law for his dereliction of royal duty, still less could she forgive the tragedy of her husband's premature death, hastened by the strain of a kingly role he did not want.

David had not entirely given up hope of having Wallis created a Royal Highness. A new Queen in the person of a young niece might prove more amenable than his brother had been. His brother's funeral, of course, was no time to raise the matter, but later that year he again journeyed to London to see his mother, whose health was failing fast. His visit coincided with Elizabeth and Philip's fifth wedding anniversary and they invited him to a celebration luncheon. Harry and Alice were there too. But if David's niece was new to the throne, her advisers were the same experienced heads who had advised her father. Nor did she herself see any reason to do something which her father, however reluctantly, had considered best left undone, and Uncle David returned to Paris disappointed.

Bertie's widow and his two daughters assuaged their grief in different ways. The widowed Elizabeth sought solitude and the comfort of memories. The elder daughter had the non-stop work of monarchy to keep her from dwelling too much on the past. The younger daughter turned more and more to Peter Townsend.

From the outset, the new Queen modelled herself on her dead father, though there was no need for her to have done so – she was already so like him in so many ways. 'While she lives, the King will never be dead,' muttered a courtier on one occasion when Elizabeth II had shown that she was very much her father's daughter. Both privately and publicly, she sought to keep his memory alive. She worked at his desk with his photograph watching her, the one taken with his small grandson to mark the boy's third birthday. She flatly turned down a suggestion that the entrance to Buckingham Palace known as the King's Door should be re-named the Queen's Door. Equally she turned down the idea that the King's Troop of the Royal Horse Artillery should now be the Queen's Troop. If she could not perpetuate the royal name of George, as her father had done in memory of his father, she could, and did, change her own surname and that of her two children from Mountbatten to Windsor. It seems to have been Churchill who, perhaps for reasons of his own, first put the idea into her head. Philip's pride was hurt, of course. If he raised little protest, it was because he, like his wife, was young and inexperienced in the workings of monarchy. His Uncle Dickie was more loudly indignant, but forced to be content with the fact that his House of Mountbatten, however briefly, had taken its place, as he put it, 'among the reigning Houses of the United Kingdom'.

However there was one thing the new Queen could not bring herself to do. She could not work in what had been her father's old room at the palace. It was too full of memories. Instead, she took over what had been her mother's sitting room and had her father's desk transferred from one to the other.

Indeed, she had no great wish to return to Buckingham Palace at all. She liked the place as little now as she had done in childhood and would have much preferred to stay on in the cosier, more intimate atmosphere of Clarence House. She and Philip talked things over and came up with the suggestion that they should keep Clarence House on as their home with the Queen commuting along the Mall to Buckingham Palace to work. Churchill shook his head. The Monarch should live at the palace, he advised. Reluctantly, they moved over, changing homes with her widowed mother.

Remembering how she herself had felt as a child when her parents had moved from Piccadilly to the palace, how she had longed for a secret tunnel so that she could slip back to her old home to sleep at night, Elizabeth did her best to arrange things so that her own children were unsettled as little as possible. When the family went to Windsor for Easter as usual, they left from Clarence House. They returned to London to Buckingham Palace. In the interval, what had once been her and Margo's old nursery at the palace, and since used by Margaret as bedroom and sitting room, had again become a nursery for her own children. And a nursery which looked just like the one at Clarence House . . . the same chintz curtains at the windows, the same furnishings, the same books and toys. Even Harvey had been thought of. Harvey was Charles's pet rabbit, a fluffy Angora. His hutch was now tucked away in a secluded corner of the palace garden.

The children, laughing and chattering as children will, and sometimes squabbling, were a considerable comfort to their widowed 'Granny' – to distinguish her from 'Gan-Gan' Queen Mary – during the months she stayed on at the palace while Clarence House was readied for her occupancy. Charles in particular. So often and in so many ways he reminded her of her beloved Bertie. The similarity between grandson and dead grandfather was to grow as Charles grew, forging a special link between grandmother and the oldest of her grandchildren.

But a grieving heart also craves solitude. Bertie's widow sought solitude that summer in Scotland, at the home of her old friend, Lady Doris Vyner, almost as far north as

111

you can get in Britain without falling over the edge. It was while there, journeying between Thurso and John o' Groats one day, that she first saw the ruins of Barrogill Castle (or the Castle of Mey, as it is now known). Perhaps its sorry state of cracked stonework and a neglected wilderness of a garden reflected her own mood of grief. Perhaps she saw its restoration as something to occupy her mind and offset grief. Perhaps she saw it as a retreat from the world. Whatever the reason, it was a spur-of-the-moment decision to buy it and plunge into the work of restoration. Arranging its repair, shopping for antiques to furnish it and local landscapes to hang on the walls, these things helped her to overcome the trauma of grief even if restoring the grounds from wilderness to garden inevitably reminded her of those early, happy days of marriage when she and the dead Bertie had similarly turned wilderness into garden at Royal Lodge.

So the re-named Castle of Mey served its purpose even if it never became the hideaway home as which she may originally have seen it. She was to visit it often in the future, but they were to be only visits, a week or so at a time, no more. Clarence House, her daughter's old home, was to become her real home, with Royal Lodge a continuing weekend retreat full of memories which, with the passage of time, became happy rather than sad. Few people outside the family were ever to penetrate the privacy of Royal Lodge, where she kept her dead husband's desk just as it had been in his lifetime. Set out on it were his leather-bound blotter, his silver inkstand, his travelling clock, and his favourite photographs, including one of herself in those long-ago days of their courtship when she had worn her hair in a fringe . . . just as though, at any moment, he might come in from the garden to settle himself at it as he had done so often in lifetime.

Poignant memories stabbed her at times in those early days of widowhood and never more so than when she went again to Sandringham that Christmas with her elder

The Queen as a small princess, with Grandpapa England (King George V) and Gan Gan (Queen Mary). 1932

The Queen at the christening of her first grandchild, Princess Anne's son, Peter Phillips. 1977

The Queen's parents, then Duke and Duchess of York, appear on the balcony at Buckingham Palace on their wedding day. 1923

The Prince and Princess of Wales on their wedding day. With them, Catherine Cameron Princess Margaret's daughter, Sarah Armstrong-Jones, and the Duke of Kent's son, Nicholas. 1981

The Queen and Prince Philip on their way from Broadlands to Romsey Abbey, Hampshire, during their honeymoon. 1947

The Queen Mother and Prince Charles leave St George's Chapel, Windsor, in an open carriage after an Order of the Garter ceremony. 1979

Princess Margaret with Lord Snowdon and their two children, Viscount Linley and Lady Sarah Armstrong-Jones, not long before the breakup of their marriage. 1978

The Queen's cousins Eddy and Alex, the Duke of Kent and his sister, Princess Alexandra, watch Lester Piggott win the 1977 Derby. With them are the Queen Mother, Princess Alexandra's husband, Angus Ogilvy, and the Duchess of Kent.

The Queen says goodbye to the Duchess of Windsor after visiting her Uncle David, the Duke of Windsor, who died ten days later. 1972

Prince Charles, his 'honorary grandfather' Earl Mountbatten and Prince Philip at a polo match. 1978

The Queen's cousin Richard and his Danish-born wife, the Duke and Duchess of Gloucester, with their three children at the christening of their daughter Lady Rose Victoria Birgitte Louise Windsor. 1980

The Queen's aunt, Princess Alice, the Dowager Duchess of Gloucester, at the christening of her grandchild Rose. 1980

...ncess Michael of Kent leaving hospital after the birth of her daughter, Lady Gabriela, ...h her husband, Prince Michael of Kent, and their son, Lord Frederick. 1981

...ce Charles and Prince Philip take a back seat to Her Majesty The Queen, the ...cess of Wales with the young Prince William, and the Queen Mother on the ...sion of the baby's christening, August 4th 1982.

The Prince and Princess of Wales on tour in the principality. 1981

daughter and son-in-law and her two small grandchildren. Several times she slipped away from the rest of the family to walk alone in the grounds where she had walked so often with her beloved Bertie. There had been one occasion, not much more than a year before, when the two of them had strolled out through a side gate and walked as far as the main Norwich Gates where a small group of hopeful sightseers were standing. 'Fancy,' Bertie had said on their return. 'Not a soul recognised us.' Now all that was past and her elder daughter had taken the father's place, making the Christmas broadcast he used to make, giving out Christmas gifts to the servants and estate workers. On Christmas Day the widowed Elizabeth sent for those few servants who had been especially close to her dead husband. To each of them she gave a gold pen engraved with her dead husband's GVIR cypher. Bertie had ordered them as gifts the previous Christmas, but had been too ill to give them out. Now his widow did so for him. 'I thought you might like these to remind you of the King,' she said.

In the family gathering at Sandringham that Christmas there were three Queens – the new Queen Elizabeth II, her mother, also Queen Elizabeth, and her grandmother, Queen Mary. Occasionally this caused a degree of confusion among the servants. Margaret, coming downstairs one day, asked a passing footman where the Queen was.

'Which Queen, Your Royal Highness?' the man queried.

'There is only one Queen,' said Margaret, loftily.

If Margaret had turned to Peter Townsend for comfort in the aftermath of her father's death, he too was now in need of comfort. His wartime marriage was disintegrating rapidly, though he and his wife Rosemary, mother of his two small sons, Giles and Hugo, kept up a brave front almost to the end. The Queen and Philip, the day they accompanied Margaret on a visit to Adelaide Cottage, the Townsends' grace-and-favour home at Windsor, can have

113

had no idea that within six months the Townsend marriage would end in divorce. At Sandringham and Windsor, in the months which followed, love finally blossomed between Margaret and Townsend.

His divorce was granted on the grounds of Rosemary's misconduct. Being the innocent party would probably not have helped much in Bertie's day. And certainly not in Grandpapa England's day. Both would have sent him on his way. But times and attitudes were changing and Queen Elizabeth II kept him on as Deputy Master of the Household. She liked Townsend, as her father had done. He had been 'Peter' to her for years. Her mother liked him too and found herself leaning on him more and more in those early days of her widowhood. So when, with Margaret, she changed homes with her elder daughter, moving from Buckingham Palace to Clarence House, she suggested taking him with her. The Queen had no objection and Townsend became the widowed mother's Comptroller, a sort of major domo, living in and working from a small house jammed between Clarence House and St James's Palace.

It was shortly after this that Margaret told first her mother and then her sister that she was in love with Peter. Her mother, though understanding, was no more convinced that marriage was possible than she had been at the time David said he was in love with Wallis. Her sister, though sympathetic enough, was deeply perturbed. Philip, when the Queen told him, tried to make a joke of it.

Townsend himself told Tommy Lascelles, the private secretary the new Queen had inherited from her dead father. Lascelles was a courtier of the old school. He still dressed in the fashions of the 1920s and his principles had the same roots. He was outraged by what Townsend told him. 'You must be either mad or bad,' he retorted.

Lascelles' advice to the Queen was that Townsend must go. But she could not, as yet, bring herself to accept that advice. Close as she was to her sister, sympathetic to her,

114

liking Townsend as she did, she closed her eyes to the problem and hoped that it would go away.

Margaret's love for Townsend was only one of a number of things which troubled the Queen at this time. The father to whom she was so devoted had died not long since. Gan Gan too was dying. And her marriage to Philip no longer glided along quite as smoothly as it had done in earlier days. He had not adapted to monarchy as quickly and easily as she had done herself, and sometimes felt a depressed and very frustrated man.

The cause of Philip's frustration and depression lay in the vastly changed circumstances of their married life. Until now, his life had always been a busy and active one. Suddenly he found himself with too little to do. At least, little that a man of his outlook and temperament could regard as worthwhile and meaningful. In the Navy he had been boss of his own ship. In marriage, previously, he had been very much head of the family. His wife, even as a Princess deputising for her sick father, had always leaned on him, turning to him for support and advice. Accession to the throne had changed all that. While he had too little to do, monarchy absorbed most of her waking hours. It meant that there were others to support and advise her. Philip felt himself frozen out.

A study of the life of Prince Albert, his predecessor in the role of consort, did little to help. Great-great-grandfather Albert had acted as Victoria's private secretary and principal adviser until he was almost playing king to her queen. More than a century later, there was no possibility of his great-great-grandson doing the same. Victoria may have been delighted to go through the contents of her 'boxes' with her beloved Albert; to have him standing by her and joining in things when the prime minister came to call. Her great-great-granddaughter had neither the desire nor the freedom to do so.

Lacking a proper job of royal work, Philip set about creating a worthwhile role on his own account. He was quick to spot that the way Buckingham Palace was run was less efficient and economic than it could be. He came up with ideas for equipping the palace with its own laundry and bakery. Both would doubtless have saved money in the long run, but were ruled out because of the capital expenditure involved. Further frustration for Philip.

He had more success at Sandringham, that sentimental white elephant which had long been a drain on the family's private purse. The Queen's great-grandfather, the spendthrift Edward VII, had not bothered what the place cost to run. Grandpapa England had been more economic, but not much. David, during his brief spell of ownership, had thought of selling it. The war years had forced economies on Bertie and, as a result, the estate was beginning to look run-down and threadbare. Rather than economise further, Philip set about devising ways and means whereby it might pay its way by producing more timber, bacon, crops for canning and freezing. What was left of his time he filled by learning to fly, something he had long wanted to do. Again, he found himself up against opposition, from Churchill and others. Before you knew where you were, they muttered among themselves, the man would be wanting to take his wife up for a flip. And his wife was the Queen. Far too dangerous. But Philip was beginning to learn that if he stuck out long enough he could get his own way.

Elizabeth did what she could to ease her husband's sense of frustration and depression. In their private life together she continued to treat him as head of the family. Children's questions were referred to him. 'Ask Papa,' she would tell them. 'He'll know.' Similarly with friends. 'I must ask Philip', she would say. As far as possible, she would down the tools of monarchy promptly at five o'clock each day to revert to her other roles as wife and mother, even asking the prime minister to postpone his weekly consultation until after the children had been put to bed.

At five o'clock, for the next ninety minutes or so,

husband and wife would join in games of hide-and-seek with the children. Or play an improvised game of football with them in the red-carpeted corridor. Or Philip would take young Charles along to the indoor pool for a swimming lesson. There would be naval manoeuvres with toy boats in the bath, bedroom romps and bedtime stories until it was time for the children to settle down and say their prayers. 'God bless Mummy and Papa, Granny and Aunt Margo.'

Even so, there was less time for family fun than there had been, and no question of having further children. Elizabeth had said earlier that she wanted a family of four, two boys and two girls. It was beginning to look as if she would have to settle for two.

She adapted to the grander, stylised atmosphere of palace life more quickly than her husband, accepting that, as Queen, she could no longer expect the comparative informality of the old days when she had been part-time Princess and part-time Navy wife. But if she accepted the fact that they could so seldom be completely alone together, that there was nearly always someone else around, Philip did not. The constant comings and goings of royal aides, pages and footmen irritated him.

To give themselves a small extra degree of privacy, they conceived the idea of 'all-in' meals. Except when entertaining guests, they would serve themselves at meal-times instead of having servants to wait on them, conversing while they ate with no one to hear what was said. The food was left on hot-plates to keep warm. At breakfast time Elizabeth would brew a pot of tea and Philip designed an electric kettle mounted on a swivel stand to make the task of pouring easier. He also bought an electric pan in which to fry bacon and eggs. Unfortunately, the smell of frying not only permeated the other rooms of the apartment, but tended to linger on. Hardly the thing when the next-door sitting room was also the Queen's study with royal aides constantly coming and going. So the frying pan did not last long.

Another idea they devised in the hope of obtaining

privacy was to use one of the towers at Windsor Castle as a sort of weekend cottage, taking only a bare minimum of staff along with them. But if Philip was happy enough to fry his own breakfast bacon, royal servants were not willing to do the same. Nor were they happy about being asked to make their own beds. On their first informal weekend at Windsor the royal couple took along only four servants. In no time at all, four had become fourteen and there was little more privacy to be obtained at Windsor than at the palace.

At Marlborough House, just down the road from Buckingham Palace, Gan Gan was dying. Carefully, she revised her will, so that what would have gone to Bertie went now to Lilibet. Dutifully, she insisted that neither her ill-health nor death if it came should be permitted to interfere with the coronation of the granddaughter she had coached so assiduously for so many years. As May of Teck, Princess of Wales, Queen Consort to Grandpapa England and Queen Mother, she had seen six monarchs on the throne, from the matriarchal Victoria to the youthful Elizabeth II. More than anything, she said, she hoped to survive long enough to see her granddaughter crowned, if only on television. But it was not to be. She died only ten weeks before the date set for the coronation.

But if she did not live to see the actual coronation ceremony, she may – at least accordinging to servants who worked for the family at the time – have seen her granddaughter with the crown on her head. In the weeks preceding her grandmother's death, Elizabeth II visited her several times at Marlborough House. With Churchill's connivance (so the story runs), on one of these occasions the crown was taken there from the Tower of London at the same time . . . and briefly donned so that Gan Gan might die happy at having seen her granddaughter 'crowned'.

10

Heartbreak for Margaret

In accordance with Queen Mary's dying wish, the coronation of her granddaughter took place as planned. David came over from Paris for his mother's funeral, but not for his niece's crowning. To the relief of some members of the family, he still took it as an insult that the invitation should have been made out to him as a Royal Highness but to Wallis only as 'Her Grace the Duchess of Windsor'. But if David was further affronted, the new Queen's Germanic in-laws were delighted to find themselves included in the official guest list. The whole tribe was invited to Britain for the occasion, sisters-in-law, their husbands, Philip's numerous nieces and nephews. And not only invited to the official ceremony, but hosted at a family dinner party at the palace.

For most of the family, the coronation was an occasion charged with high emotion. Young Charles was perhaps a notable exception. At four, he was more thrilled by a new hair dressing which had been used to keep his hair in place. 'Smell, Granny,' he urged his grandmother. 'Doesn't it smell nice?'

Overcome by the emotion of the moment, the new Queen found herself wiping away tears as the state coach carried her to her crowning. Philip was so tense and strung-up that he nearly dislodged the crown while paying homage to his wife as her 'liege man of life and

119

limb'. Margaret bubbled with excitement like a newly-opened bottle of champagne and a single small incident, brought on by the excitement of the moment, betrayed her feelings for Peter Townsend.

It happened just after the ceremony. Her sister had climbed back into the state coach for the long roundabout processional drive to Buckingham Palace. Attendant footmen rolled up the length of her coronation robe and deposited it, like a roll of carpet, on the opposite seat, its gold cypher facing her. The drive to the Abbey had already given the Queen some experience of the way the coach swayed on its leather braces and she asked for the cypher to be turned away from her. 'I don't want to be seasick,' she said.

The massive four-ton coach lumbered on its way through the pelting rain. Margaret and others waited in the Abbey entrance until it was their turn to leave. Peter Townsend was with her. She spied a stray piece of cotton on the breast pocket of his Air Force uniform. She picked it off. Then, looking up into his eyes, laughing, she brushed her hand affectionately along his row of medals, Distinguished Service Order, Distinguished Flying Cross and Bar among them.

That small intimate gesture told the world what her sister and mother and only one or two others already knew: that she was in love with Peter Townsend.

Just as at the time of her Uncle David's abdication, American newspapers were first with the story. And just as at the time of the abdication, Britain's newspapers, however reluctantly, held back. But they would not keep silent for ever and the prospect of another royal love scandal at the outset of a new reign horrified those whose duty it was to advise the young Queen.

Their fears were realised less than two weeks later when a Sunday newspaper denied the whole story. To do so, of course, it first had to repeat what it was denying. Now that things were out in the open, Tommy Lascelles reiterated his advice that Townsend must be sent away. Churchill was called into consultation. He was devoted to the young Queen and she may have hoped that he would find a way out for her in her personal dilemma over her sister and Townsend. Churchill, as prime minister, felt bound to reinforce the advice she had already been given by Lascelles. There could no longer be any question of playing for time. Reluctantly, Elizabeth felt obliged to accept the advice she was given and act upon it.

Her mother and sister were about to leave on a tour of what was then Southern Rhodesia. Peter Townsend, as Comptroller at Clarence House, had masterminded the arrangements for the trip and was to have gone with them. Out of the blue, he was suddenly ordered to remain behind and instead of going to Southern Rhodesia with Margaret and her mother, he was detailed to accompany Elizabeth and Philip on their post-coronation visit to Northern Ireland.

And that was only the thin end of what was to prove a very large wedge. Margaret left for Southern Rhodesia upset, but still hopeful. She was young, in love and love would surely find a way. Peter Townsend, older and wiser in the ways of the world, was less surprised to find that that visit to Northern Ireland would be his last royal chore. To him, the real surprise was that he had not been asked to go earlier. Now that the moment had finally come, he was given the post of a British air attaché and a choice of three postings: Brussels, Johannesburg or Singapore. He picked Brussels as being nearest both to Margaret and the two young sons of his broken marriage.

Margaret was heartbroken when news of his departure from Britain reached her in Umtali. She had been promised, she thought – indeed, they both did – that he would not have to leave until she was back and had seen him again. She cancelled her engagements for the following day and shut herself in her room. The traditional royal excuse of 'a cold' was trotted out for public consumption.

By the time she returned to Britain, Peter Townsend was already in Brussels.

Margaret felt she had been handed a rather raw deal. And, judged by the less hidebound standards of a later generation, perhaps she had. With Townsend's departure, her personality underwent a considerable metamorphosis. No longer was she the carefree, impulsive younger sister, mischievous in private, sparkling in public. That side of her personality was to return . . . to ebb and flow with the ups and downs of her private life. In the immediate aftermath of losing Townsend, she became something of a recluse, pining for her lost love. She kept her favourite photograph of him, one showing him in Air Force uniform, close to her always. They wrote to each other regularly; indulged in long, lingering telephone calls. Love, Margaret continued to hope, would still find a way.

Christmas that year found her at Sandringham as usual, with her mother. Elizabeth and Philip were not there. They were away on a six-months tour of the Commonwealth which was to take them right round the world. If the tour with its crowded schedule of receptions, balls, banquets, garden parties, children's displays, speeches and hand-shakes, was hardly a vacation, it provided Philip at least with a welcome break from the frustrations of palace life. At sea aboard the liner *Gothic* – the new royal yacht *Britannia* was not yet in service – he became a different man, extrovert and dominant, a demon player of deck hockey, a boisterous barber's assistant in a striped apron, his nose reddened with grease-paint, on the day of crossing the equator.

Elizabeth missed the children. Wherever she slept she had their photographs beside her on a bedside table. She wrote to them often; sent them picture postcards from the various ports of call. On Christmas Day she put in a radio-telephone call from New Zealand to Sandringham, where they were spending Christmas with Granny and Aunt Margo, to talk to them.

Among the children's Christmas presents that year, as every year throughout childhood, was a bulging Christmas stocking apiece made by mummy before she left, discarded nylons filled with childish knick-knacks. There was a similar home-made Christmas stocking too for each of the pet corgis, filled with such doggy delights as balls and biscuits and rubber bones. Among other gifts for the boy Charles was a swashbuckling outfit which included a velvet cloak and a toy sword. They became the props for a game based on what he had seen at Westminster Abbey some months previous. 'We're playing coronations,' he explained. 'I am the King and Anne is the Queen.' A tablecloth draped about his sister's shoulders did duty as a coronation robe.

Young as Charles was, he had already started lessons. His mother had been teaching him to spell, count and tell the time. In her absence, lessons continued under Mispy, as he and Anne called Katherine Peebles, the young Scots governess the Queen had engaged before leaving on her prolonged tour. Granny doted on her grandchildren and was inclined to spoil them, as grandmothers will. Bedtime, with her around, was inclined to vary. 'Oh, let them have just a little longer,' she would plead when Nanny Lightbody bustled in to say that it was time for bed.

The children's upbringing, under Mrs Lightbody's supervision, was firmly based on routine. Except when Granny was around to intervene, fixed hours and regular mealtimes were a must. Few food fads were permitted, sweets were rationed and none at all were allowed until after lunch for fear of spoiling childish appetites. Cleanliness, punctuality and politeness were drilled into them, politeness to such an extent that the children would say 'please' and 'thank you' even when training their pet corgis.

Originally, there had been only one corgi, Susan, who went everywhere with the children's mother, even on honeymoon. Later Susan was joined by her daughter,

Sugar. She in turn produced pups, two of which, Whisky and Sherry, were given to the children as their special pets. And so on and so forth until, in time, there were to be half-a-dozen or more frisking and snapping about the palace.

Charles's response to childhood upbringing was genteel obedience. He did nothing without asking permission first. Anne did first and asked afterwards. She was the dominant one, active and lively, always dancing and singing and rushing around. Mealtimes were about the only occasions when she sat still for more than a minute at a time. She was the venturesome one too, something of a tomboy, preferring toy guns to dolls, forever teasing her brother, occasionally putting on a display of tantrums which would merit, and receive, a corrective spanking from Papa.

With the new royal yacht ready for sea at last, the two children became the first of the family to sail on it when it set out to rendezvous with their parents at Tobruk. They were accorded a guard of honour when they went aboard, with the more confident Anne saying a jaunty, 'How do you do?' to each sailor in turn. Not to be outdone, Charles, when they were at last reunited with their parents, greeted his mother with a small outstretched hand. 'Oh, no – not you, darling,' she told him, hugging and kissing both children, overjoyed to see them again.

There was a load of toys for the children which the parents had been given in the course of their travels. It was typical of Anne that she should be more excited by her brother's working model of Gibraltar than by her own dolls' house. Father, too, was keen to operate the Gibraltar model with its miniature railway. With the children, Philip often became a child again himself, playing games of cowboys and Indians with them in the palace shrubberies, changing into swimming trunks and joining them for a splash in the fountain in the days before Windsor had its own swimming pool. At Balmoral he would take them off on camping expeditions, cooking them barbecue meals and spending the night in sleeping bags in an isolated lodge by the edge of Loch Muick.

In many ways Elizabeth quickly proved herself a born Queen, dutiful, conscientious and hard-working, taking to monarchy as a a duck takes to water. The public side of things she found less acceptable, sometimes jibbing at what Philip laughingly referred to as 'dressing up and queening it'. Public appearances, particularly those involving a display of jewelled ornaments, made her tense and nervous. She was happiest and most relaxed away from the public eye, crown and robe replaced by headscarf and tweeds, pursued not by a string of courtiers, but by a frisk of corgis or a lollop of Labradors. Had a twist of fate (in the shape of her uncle's abdication) not brought her to the throne, she would probably have done what her daughter Anne has done since marriage, retreating into the country and surrounding herself with dogs, horses and children.

With so many servants around, only a genuinely 'doggy' person would have continued to feed the corgis each day, as Elizabeth did, mixing the meat, biscuit and gravy herself with a silver fork before doling it out into the feeding bowls. At Balmoral, if one of the dogs showed a tendency to scratch after a run on the moors, she would kneel down and investigate until the cause of the scratching was found and removed. At Sandringham, walking the dogs on one occasion, she came to an area where farm-workers were threshing corn. She paused and lifted the dogs, one by one, over the intervening wire-mesh fence to have a go at the rats. In doing so, she somehow lost the minute gold and platinum wristwatch she had been given as a small girl. It was only later, on her way back to the house, that she discovered the loss. Immediately she hurried back to search for the lost watch in the falling dusk. Without success. The search was resumed the following day and continued for almost a week, but the watch was never found.

As with dogs, so with horses. With her father's death, the toy horses she and Margaret had so carefully groomed in childhood had been replaced by an inherited string of racehorses. Racing became her great passion and the *Sporting Life* required reading. Journeys to Sandringham were interrupted by an early-morning stop at Newmarket to see her horses in training and race days, if she had a horse running, would invariably find her in the paddock conversing with her jockey.

Her big ambition was, and is, to win the Derby. She came close to that with Aureole in the year of her coronation, but a good-luck pat from a passing racegoer upset the unpredictable colt to the extent of costing her the race. So it was with fingers crossed that Elizabeth went to Ascot to see Aureole run in the prestigious King George VI and Queen Elizabeth Stakes soon after returning from her Commonwealth tour. Initially it seemed that she was doomed to witness a repetition of the previous year's Derby. Before the race started Aureole shied and unseated his jockey. The off found him swerving right across the course, losing ground until he was at the tail-end of the field. With a mile still to go, he settled to the race, gaining ground and moving up through the field. In the royal box, Elizabeth found it impossible to restrain her excitement as Aureole hit the front. She shouted a string of instructions her jockey could not possibly have heard: 'Stay in front. Keep riding.' She hopped frantically from one foot to the other, clapping her white-gloved hands in delight as Aurole passed the winning post first. 'We've done it. We've done it,' she exclaimed excitedly to those around her.

'I've never seen you so excited,' her mother told her.

Different in temperament though they were in many ways, mother and elder daughter continued to share a closely affectionate relationship. Regularly each morning, before settling at her desk to tackle the routine chores of monarchy, the daughter would telephone the mother at

126

Clarence House to chat of this and that. Mum at this time was usually still in bed, propped up with pillows as she tackled her correspondence in a more leisurely fashion. She was never the slave to the clock her husband had been. Time and again in his lifetime, Bertie could have been found pacing impatiently up and down as he waited for her to accompany him somewhere, fretting more and more as the minutes ticked away, taking it out on those around him, but instantly forgiving the moment she finally appeared on the scene with her warm smile and abundant charm. The Queen, her father's daughter in punctuality as in so much else, quickly devised an antidote to her mother's more casual attitude to time-keeping, a variation of Grandpapa England's idea of 'Sandringham time'. If she could not set the clocks half an hour fast, as her grandfather had done at Sandringham, she could tell her mother, upon occasion, that meals, outings and so forth were half an hour earlier than was actually the case.

Mother and daughter were not only closely affectionate, but also closely companionable, often together at the races, at Balmoral and Sandringham, seeing each other almost every weekend at Windsor. The Queen's decision in the matter of Peter Townsend had not come between them. Fond as she was of her younger daughter, understanding as she was of Margaret's love for Townsend, the Queen Mother had too many memories of the abdication not to realise that her elder daughter had done the only thing that could be done.

But what Elizabeth had done in the matter of Townsend had served only to afford a breathing space. Margaret still loved him, was still set on marrying him, still sure that love and time would find a way. There was a briefly romantic reunion for the ill-starred lovers just before Margaret's twenty-fourth birthday. A cloak and dagger operation saw Townsend flying from Brussels to Britain under a pseudonym (which he later explained was due

127

simply to a booking error), meeting a royal aide in the book department at Harrods and being driven from there to Clarence House for a secret meeting with Margaret.

But it was the following year, the year of Margaret's twenty-fifth birthday, that matters came finally to a head.

Margaret's twenty-fifth birthday seemed to offer a way out of the unhappy romantic situation in which she had been trapped for so long. At twenty-five she was no longer quite so hamstrung by the legal complexities of the Royal Marriages Act which her long-dead ancestor, George III, had pushed through Parliament after two of his brothers had contracted what he considered to be 'scandalous marriages' with commoners. It would still be nice to have her sister's queenly consent, of course, but failing that, she could give the Privy Council twelve months' notice of her intention to marry and then go ahead provided Parliament raised no objection.

Seven weeks after her twenty-fifth birthday Townsend again returned to Britain, moving into a Knightsbridge apartment loaned to him by the Marquess of Abergavenny, a close friend of the Royals. That same night Margaret left Scotland, where she had been staying with her mother, and travelled to London by overnight train. In the privacy of Clarence House she and Peter were again reunited. That weekend, with the world's press hard on their heels, they fled London for the comparative peace and quiet of the country home of Margaret's cousin, Jean Lycett Wills, daughter of her mother's sister, Lady Elphinstone. But peace and quiet was possible only inside the house. Outside, the place was besieged by reporters and photographing helicopters buzzed overhead.

Two years of separation had done nothing to diminish Margaret's love for Peter Townsend. She still wanted to marry him and the problem which the Queen had hoped would go away now confronted her again with appalling cruelty. As sister, she wanted only Margaret's happiness. Michael Adeane had replaced Tommy Lascelles as her private secretary and Anthony Eden, himself divorced and remarried, was now prime minister. But the advice she received from them both was the same as that given by Lascelles and Churchill. As Queen and Defender of the Faith, she could not give regal consent to a marriage between her sister, at that time third in succession to the throne, and a divorced man, however innocent. As for Margaret going ahead without the Queen's consent, well that was perhaps possible if she renounced her right of succession to the throne, sacrificed her official allowance and withdrew into private life. For her to do so would require a special parliamentary Bill in both Britain and the countries of the Commonwealth, and Eden discussed the matter with Cabinet colleagues. Prominent among those opposed to the idea was the Marquess of Salisbury, as rigid in matters of royal principle as that ancestor who advised the first Elizabeth. He spoke in terms of resignation rather than see such a Bill introduced in the House of Lords.

In the family circle, Margaret stood alone – just as her Uncle David had done all those years before. Others of the family were more sympathetic to her than they had been to him, but all were more or less equally set against marriage to Townsend. Uncle Harry shook his head as firmly as he had done over the question of his brother's marriage to Wallis Simpson. Even the Queen Mother, much as she loved her younger daughter and desired her happiness, fond as she was of Townsend, could not bring herself to endorse a marriage of which she knew the dead Bertie would never have approved. Among her contemporaries in the family Margaret found no greater support. Her sister, as Queen, had to say 'No' while her brother-in-law, Philip, no longer saw the proposed marriage as a joking matter but as something which could only 'diminish the dignity of the Crown'.

Townsend was not with Margaret when she went to Windsor the following weekend (though he had seen her again only the evening before) to make one last appeal to her sister. Philip was there too and the three of them had dinner together. Sympathetic to Margaret as she still was, the Queen remained firm. As Queen, she could hardly fly in the face of the advice tendered to her. And while she could not, would not, do anything which might hinder Margaret from going ahead of her own accord, she could not approve of that either. And if she did go ahead of her own accord, Margaret should clearly realise the implications. At the very least, she would have to sacrifice her right of succession and her official allowance to have any hope of obtaining parliamentary approval. Married (if she did succeed in obtaining approval), she might not have to live on love alone, but it would certainly be a question of living on Peter's pay-packet. As the family conference went on, the hopelessness of her situation dawned more and more on Margaret and by the end of the evening she was in tears.

Next day she talked to Peter on the telephone. What she told him concerning what her sister and Philip had said merely served to confirm his own worst fears. There was simply no way out. Replacing the telephone, he sat down and began drafting the statement with which Margaret was shortly to renounce him. Margaret herself told her sister and mother that she and Peter had finally decided not to pursue things further. Both were distressed for her, but also considerably relieved.

The statement of renunciation which Townsend drafted for Margaret could have been issued almost immediately. Instead, for some reason, those around the Queen counselled a few days' delay. So, as far as the rest of the world was concerned, the love story of Margaret and Townsend was still open-ended when they again spent the following weekend together, this time at the home of Lord Rupert Nevill, a close friend of the Royals, and his wife Micky. There was even a rumour among the besieging pressmen that the ill-starred lovers were planning an elopement.

Few people at that time knew the truth: that for Margaret and Peter Townsend there was to be no fairytale ending. Their love for each other may have survived two years of separation, but it could not face up to the harsh realities which marriage would entail.

On Monday 31 October, at Clarence House, they said goodbye to each other. Later that evening Margaret issued the 'statement of renunciation' which Townsend had drafted for her. 'I would like it to be known that I have decided not to marry Group Captain Peter Townsend . . . I have reached this decision entirely alone . . .' In the final analysis, perhaps she had, but the pressures, inside and outside the family, had left her no other option.

11

A New Relationship

In the four years since her husband's death, the widowed Elizabeth had regained much, if not quite all, of her old vitality and zest for life. Winston Churchill had helped to win her back to the mainstream of public life. 'The country needs you, Ma'am,' he had urged her. 'Your daughter needs you.' So the Castle of Mey, restored from a crumbling ruin to its former glory, with more comfort and elegance inside its ancient walls than previous occupants had ever known, served not as a retreat from the world but a holiday home to which from time to time she welcomed others of the family . . . her elder daughter and her husband along with Philip's mother and the children. Marina's younger son, Michael, was also in the party. It was Anne's fifth birthday and Granny staged a surprise party along with a farewell firework display to celebrate the occasion.

To distinguish between her and her elder daughter, royal aides now referred to her as Queen Elizabeth while her daughter was simply The Queen. To the public she was the Queen Mother, a title which her servants abridged to the more affectionate 'Queen Mum'. She knew what they called her and took it as a tribute. She was Mummy to her daughters and Granny to her grandchildren. She was devoted to them and took time out on an official tour of the United States to go shopping for toys in

New York. She bought Anne a toy washing machine and Charles a model steam shovel.

Tours abroad and a renewed flurry of public engagements at home kept her busy as she moved into the second half of her fifties. Keeping busy prevented her from dwelling too much on the past. She still thought of Bertie, often, but time was beginning to dull the ache of memory.

In the spring of 1956 she travelled north to Liverpool to see her horse Devon Loch run in the Grand National. As always when she went racing, she was equipped for every conceivable variation of Britain's uncertain weather, taking with her three coats (fur, tweed and rain), boots and overshoes, umbrella, foot muff, rug and hot-water bottle. Her two daughters were both with her, hopping with excitement, as Devon Loch, the 100–7 second favourite for the race, cleared the massive jumps in fine style and led the way home by a clear five–six lengths.

It seemed all over bar the shouting and back in London, at Clarence House, her page switched off the television set and rushed out to collect the proceeds of his winning bet. But there were to be no winnings for him to collect and at Liverpool the Queen Mum and her two daughters could only stare in amazement and dismay as Devon Loch suddenly stopped and went down, spread-eagled. By the time jockey Dick Francis had the horse on its feet again they had been passed by every other mount still left in the race.

Mother and daughters were bitterly disappointed. But disappointed though she was, the Queen Mum was more concerned for jockey and horse. She commiserated with Dick Francis and gave Devon Loch a consoling pat. 'You dear poor old boy,' she said to him.

Margaret, in contrast, was a long way from recapturing the high-spirited vitality of her earlier years. She was still pining for Peter Townsend and had not yet – despite her public statement of renunciation – finally given up hope of one day marrying him. She spent a great deal of time brooding in the privacy of her room at Clarence House and sought comfort in religion. The wedding of two old friends, Colin Tennant and Anne Coke, to which she was invited the following month, stirred painful memories and she sat through the ceremony looking pale and distant. The wedding took place at Holkham in Norfolk, not many miles from Sandringham. An up-and-coming young photographer from London was imported to take the wedding photographs. His name was Tony Armstrong-Jones. Margaret, that day, took no more notice of him than she would have done of any other photographer and neither of them can have had the slightest idea of the traumatic future which lay in store for them.

Nor was Philip entirely his old breezy, extrovert self, though he was gradually adjusting to the big change monarchy had brought to his marriage and personal life. He was busier now than he had been, with a growing number of appointments and public engagements in his own right, trying hard to make something worthwhile and meaningful of his nebulous role as his wife's Consort. Nevertheless he missed being at sea and still found palace life boring and palace protocol frustrating.

Nor was he entirely happy about the way his son, Charles, was being raised. Too many women fussing around the boy all the time; too much petticoat government. A good dose of boarding school was what was needed, Philip thought.

To his wife and mother-in-law, it seemed a rather revolutionary idea. Aunt Marina and Uncle Harry might have sent their children to school, but none of them was destined to be King one day. Future kings might go to university or into the Navy, but they did not go to school. True, there had at one time been talk of sending Elizabeth and Margaret to school, but nothing had come of it. True, the Queen Mother had been to school, but only briefly. She did not think that life at a boys' boarding school would suit her grandson, shy and nervous as he was at that time. The boy's mother was not enthusiastic about the idea either, though for a different reason: she thought that schoolboy life would expose Charles far too much to the glare of the public spotlight.

'I think people will understand and give the boy a break,' Philip argued.

He was eager for his son to be raised in his own more extrovert image and, as usual in family matters, the Queen gave way. As a first move in the chain of change, Nanny Lightbody who, Philip thought, was inclined to treat Charles more as a royal prince than a small boy, was retired to a grace-and-favour home near the Oval cricket ground. Since birth, she had been like a second mother to Charles. In fact, he had seen a good deal more of her at times than of his real mother and he was heartbroken when she went. Her going was only one of several radical changes designed to make 'a real boy' of him. The dancing classes which his mother thought so good for his deportment came to an end. Instead, he was buzzed off for physical training sessions and games of schoolboy football. And that Christmas, with his father away in the Antarctic, he found himself with a male tutor instead of a female governess.

An invitation to open the 1956 Olympic Games in Australia had presented Philip with the ideal excuse to escape the boredom and frustration of palace life for a time. He was still in his early thirties, young, eager and adventurous. His old naval buddy of wartime days, Mike Parker, now serving as his private secretary and general factotum, was around the same age and cast in the same mould, a breezy, extrovert Australian. When the Olympic Games invitation turned up, the pair of them had put their heads together and cooked up the idea of turning the trip into a real *Schoolboys' Own* adventure which, that winter, was to take them deep into the Antarctic aboard the royal yacht, visiting lonely islands and isolated outposts. They were gone for four months.

It all happened at a time when Mike Parker's wartime marriage, like Peter Townsend's before him, was heading for a breakdown. Philip's own marriage had been no hastily conceived wartime affair and, for all his frustration with palace life, was still a happy one. Elizabeth missed him desperately while he was away. If he missed her less consistently in all the excitement of shipboard life, there were times when he felt her absence acutely. Ashore in New Zealand, he spotted a picture of her, a reproduction of an Edward Halliday painting, in an hotel. He asked if he could have it and took it back aboard *Britannia* with him to hang in his cabin. The two of them spoke often by radio-telephone and, opening his gifts in mid-ocean on Christmas Day, he was delighted to discover a tape recording she had made. Playing it back in the privacy of his cabin brought echoes of home as he heard her wish him an affectionate 'Merry Christmas' along with a chorus of 'Hello, Papa' from the children and the excited woofing of the pet corgis in the background.

Philip was away on his long trip when Charles started school after Christmas. Mother and father, in their slightly differing views on the value of schoolboy life, had come to a compromise. To send him straight from the cosy confines of the palace nursery to the harsher environment of boarding school, they agreed, would be too much of a shock to the boy's system. Instead, he was first sent to a day school in London, returning home at the end of lessons for supper, bed and breakfast just as his mother had done during her brief wartime stint in the ATS.

Philip was still away, though his trip was nearing its end, when Parker's wife, Eileen, announced that she and Mike had separated. There had been gossip about them even before that, and in all the rumours which were flying around the names of the two couples, Eileen and Mike, Elizabeth and Philip, were somehow confused.

The result was a story published around the world that Liz and Phil, as the American newspapers styled them, were likewise heading for divorce.

Elizabeth was horrified and upset by the newspaper stories. 'How can they say such cruel things about us?' she sighed to Bobo MacDonald, her longtime confidante. Philip, when she spoke to him on the matter by radio-telephone, was furious. Mike Parker was aghast that his friend and employer, and, worse still, his friend's wife, the Queen, should have been drawn into the trauma of his own wrecked marriage. The only solution, he felt, was for him to distance himself from them as speedily as possible; to resign his post and quit royal service. Philip urged him to stay on. Elizabeth too, also considering herself a friend of Parker, telephoned from London to assure him that there was no need to resign. 'I feel I have to go,' Parker insisted with sacrificial loyalty. He had been with Philip for nearly ten years, masterminding his travels and public engagements, sharing his flying lessons, bolstering him through periods of frustration and depression. Now, at Gibraltar, the two friends said goodbye, shook hands and went their different ways. Parker flew back to Britain and Philip went on to Portugal where Elizabeth joined him for a state visit.

With husband and royal wife not only reunited, but clearly delighted and happy to be together again, the newspaper stories took a new turn and finally ceased. Their four months of separation proved to have been good for the couple. Together again, they were able to look at each other with fresh eyes and, with Mike Parker's failed marriage as a warning beacon, were able to see more clearly the weaknesses in their own. Almost imperceptibly they nudged their relationship along new lines, with Elizabeth no longer so totally committed to the demands of monarchy and Philip at last settling to acceptance of the fact that, where monarchy was concerned, he was first mate, not the captain.

Their marriage took on a fresh lease of life and they were full of new plans for the future. Their visit to the Queen Mother's Castle of Mey had shown them that a castle can also be an away-from-it-all retreat. Windsor Castle was a good deal larger than Mey, of course, but there seemed no reason why one of its towers should not be turned into the royal equivalent of a cottage in the country. Planning the conversion was a shared experience they both enjoyed. Like a couple of young newlyweds, they sat together evening after evening, looking through wallpaper samples, paint charts, curtain fabrics. Philip waxed enthusiastic about double-duty furniture he had seen on a trip to Canada, divans which served as beds at night and dressing tables which became desks by day. They decided to adopt the idea for the guest rooms. It was Philip too, using bits of foam rubber to represent roses, who designed a new rose garden and fountain for them to look out on while Elizabeth, unable to make up her mind about wallpaper, had her car brought round one day and drove to a shop where she could see what certain patterns looked like in the roll. She made her choice, had the wallpaper loaded into the car on the spot and drove back to the palace. The black Ford Zephyr in which she made the excursion attracted no more attention than any other car in London that day.

There was now little, if any, contact between the family in London and the 'exiled' Uncle David in Paris. If Wallis was not the Queen she may once have hoped she would become, she was concerned to ensure that her third husband should continue to live as a king. So there were liveried servants about the place and the money David and Wallis spent was always fresh from the French mint; never a used note to soil either of their fingers.

For his part, David, though he had now given up hope of seeing Wallis raised to the status of Royal Highness, which he was still convinced should automatically have been hers by virtue of his own birth, bestowed the title on her himself. She was always to be addressed as 'Your Royal Highness', he instructed the liveried servants. When one of them, newly arrived from London, addressed her on one occasion as 'Your Grace' instead, David barked angrily at him, 'You're not in England now, man.'

They travelled a great deal, though not to Britain, and the people they met on their travels were similarly expected to address Wallis as 'Your Royal Highness'. Most of those who did so, of course, had little understanding of the subtle distinction between 'Your Grace' (a duchess, which Wallis was) and 'Your Royal Highness' (a princess, which – officially – she was not), as David's niece, Elizabeth II, discovered on a stopover in New York while visiting the United States in connection with the 350th anniversary of the first British settlement at Jamestown.

In New York the VIP suite at the Waldorf Towers had been placed at her disposal. In the lobby of the suite a statuette of herself in her coronation regalia had been installed in her honour. She paused to look at it. Then, glancing up, she spotted a commemorative plaque listing the names of those who had occupied the suite before her, among them 'T.R.H. The Duke and Duchess of Windsor'. T.R.H. could stand only for 'Their Royal Highnesses' which, as far as she was concerned, her aunt by marriage was not, and her eyes reflected her displeasure.

Prior to leaving for the United States, she and Philip had personally delivered their small son to his first boarding school. Cheam was Papa's old school (though now sited at a different location) and Philip had revelled in his schoolboy life there. Charles did not like it nearly as much. Instead of his own nursery bedroom, he now found himself sharing a dormitory with nine other boys, and rather rough boys by the genteel standards to which he had been previously accustomed. There was no carpet on the floor, no heating, and the bed had wooden slats instead of springs. There was no maid to make his bed for him, no footman to clean his shoes, and he found himself doing both tasks himself. If some of this was novel enough to be something of a boyish adventure, much of it, to a youngster of Charles's tender upbringing, was rather frightening, especially the small degree of bullying to which he was occasionally subject. And no Nanny Lightbody to whom to turn for comfort. Even Hill House had had a mainly female staff, while here it was nearly all masters. Shy and introverted as he was, he would blush beetroot-red if attention was directed at him in class; shuffle his feet and stammer an answer if asked a question. Bit by bit he gained confidence and learned to stand up for himself, yet he was never really happy at Cheam, nor at that other old school of his father's, Gordonstoun, to which he was sent in due course.

Exposure to schoolboy life also exposed him to schoolboy bugs and bumps. He had tonsillitis, 'flu and chicken pox (which he passed on to Anne when he went home for the hols). A sprained ankle saw him hobbling around over Christmas with his leg in plaster. 'Hopalong Cassidy' Anne nicknamed him.

She was, at this stage of their young lives, a very different character from her brother, extrovert, pushy, much the more dominant child. Charles was nervous of horses, but not Anne. She rode them as confidently as her mother, plus something of the dash and daring Papa displayed on the polo field. At Balmoral on one occasion, copying something seen on television, she cantered bareback round and round the lawn. Her mother spotted her and called from a window, 'Get down at once, Anne, and take that horse to be properly saddled.'

She was often full of mischief and keen on teasing tricks. At Sandringham her grandmother intercepted her as she was leading her pony up the front steps with the intention of riding into the house, just as the adjutant at Sandhurst did on the day of the annual passing-out parade. At Windsor a favourite trick was to gallop full tilt at a wall far too high for her pony to clear and then, amidst

140

frightened gasps from other members of the family, bring her mount to a sliding last-moment standstill. These same traits of daring and risk-taking were to make her European eventing champion some time in the future.

Each summer, before going to Balmoral with their parents, the two children would spend a few days at Sandringham with Granny. 'Going to stay with Granny' was a treat which they eagerly anticipated. Like any other granny with any other grandchildren, she was inclined to spoil them, indulging them with ice cream at lunch time, boiled eggs for tea, chocolates at all times, letting them stay up late, reading stories to them at bedtime and giving them extra pocket-money for spending sprees. One year she bought them a pet budgerigar each. They named the birds Davy and Annie (after Davy Crockett and Annie Oakley) and taught them a few simple tricks, letting them out of their cage to flutter round the palace nursery, alighting on furniture and fingers.

Regularly each Christmas the whole family, or almost the whole family, would gather at Sandringham, just as in Bertie's day and Grandpapa England's day . . . Mummy and Papa, the two children, Granny and Aunt Margo. Marina would journey there with her brood to join them. She found the rail journey tedious and tiring, but came just the same. For Uncle Harry, Aunt Alice and their two sons, it was a shorter and easier trip from their home at Barnwell Manor, near Peterborough.

Though she was Philip's cousin, Marina was fifteen years his senior, almost of a different generation. By the time Charles first went to Cheam, her elder son, Eddy, was a young man of twenty-two, an officer in the Royal Scots Greys, looking very like the dead father from whom he had inherited his title of Duke of Kent at the tender age of six. Alex, his sister, tall and statuesque like her mother, celebrated her coming-of-age that Christmas Day of 1957, a birthday she shared with Aunt Alice. Even Michael, the wartime baby born only weeks before his father died so tragically, was now into his teens, as were the Gloucester boys, William and Richard.

It was a jolly family Christmas, marred only by the fact that the Queen had a sniffly head cold. As always, a giant Christmas tree was set up in the ballroom where Edward VII once danced with Lillie Langtry to the music of a hurdy-gurdy. Gifts in colourful wrapping paper were heaped on trestle tables set up around the tree. Among Charles's gifts one year around this time was a model train set. As is frequently also the case in less regal homes, he hardly had a look in when it came to operating it. Papa, Great-uncle Harry and the soldierly Eddy of Kent all vied with each other to show him how to work it. 'Better leave it to us. You might break it,' Charles was told. No wonder he was up at the crack of dawn next morning. A passing footman asked what he was doing about so early. 'I'm going to play with my train set,' Charles told him, adding darkly, 'if they haven't broken it for me.'

It was the same with a miniature drum kit he was given another Christmas. This was set up alongside the grand piano, with Philip and Eddy taking it in turns to bang out a rhythmic accompaniment while Marina and Margaret played the piano. Every Christmas there was a hearty singsong session round the piano, with Elizabeth and Margaret bringing back memories of their wartime amateur pantomime days as they joined together in duets like *Little White Bull*.

Elizabeth might be Queen, but Philip was always the leading light at Christmas, full of beans, busy organising games and competitions. With Marina he would devise clues for a treasure hunt which would send everyone racing along corridors, up and down stairs, in and out of rooms. A game called *He* was another favourite, and even more rumbustious, with the family splitting into two teams intent upon capturing each other, while rescuing any of their own side who might be captured by the 'enemy'. And there was always charades, a longtime

142

Royal Family favourite played in style, with hats and coats donned to portray different characters, walking sticks, riding crops and pipes used as props, and with Margaret and Elizabeth embellishing their performances with a wide range of accents, Irish, Scots, Cockney and American.

12

Sisterly Secrets

All her life the Queen had been plagued, on and off, by chills and colds. In childhood they had sometimes forced her to miss her weekly meeting of the Girl Guides. Now, in her early thirties, they seemed to be getting worse, hitting her more often and with greater severity. At Sandringham, that winter, she was forced to take to her bed at one stage with streaming eyes and a feverish temperature. Before that, for the same reason, she had been obliged to call off a weekend she and Philip had planned to spend with his cousin Patricia, Uncle Dickie's elder daughter, and her husband John, Lord Brabourne. Soon afterwards, in the April, she was again laid low at Windsor and a whole succession of visits and dinner parties had to be cancelled. She was still not really well when she attended the Windsor horse show in May and certainly should never have gone out, as she did, to play her traditional part in the Trooping the Colour ceremony on a June day of pouring rain.

Her coronation ceremony had similarly been an occasion of incessant rain, but then she had had the shelter of the state coach as she journeyed to and fro. There could be no state coach for Trooping the Colour. She would be on horseback, exposed to the elements.

'Postpone it,' Philip suggested as they looked together from one of the palace windows at the downpour outside.

Elizabeth shook her head. She pointed at the umbrellas, raincoats and plastic hoods of the crowd outside the palace. 'If they can stand the rain, then so can I,' she insisted, doggedly.

She rode side-saddle through the pouring rain to Horse Guards Parade, played her part in the traditional ceremony, rode back and sat her horse in front of the palace to take the salute. It was a triumph of majesty and dutiful obstinacy, but it did nothing to help her health. And the following month she paid the price.

She struggled her way through a tour of Scotland, but as the train carried her south again to another welter of engagements in Carlisle she had clearly reached the end of her tether. Her temperature was again feverish, her face flushed, eyes streaming and her throat swollen. Worried about her, Philip put in a telephone call to Lord Evans, her principal physician.

'Evans thinks you should get back to London immediately,' he told his wife. 'Don't worry about Carlisle. I'll handle things on my own.'

The Queen was in no condition to argue, but could only acquiesce. Philip hopped off at Carlisle on his own and the train continued south to London, where Elizabeth went straight home and straight to bed.

She was hardly the best of patients. Any slight temporary improvement would find her getting up, getting dressed and tackling the contents of her 'boxes' . . . only to have to take to her bed again a few hours later. An X-ray examination revealed a sinus condition necessitating a minor operation carried out under local anaesthetic.

Members of the family rallied round to help out and comfort her while she was incapacitated. Philip kept her company whenever he could, eating his meals at her bedside, nursing a tray on his lap. Along with her mother, he carried out public engagements on her behalf. Anne was constantly in and out to see how Mummy was doing. Margaret too would pop in from time to time.

If Margaret had not forgotten Peter Townsend, she was no longer pining for him to quite the same extent. She was getting out and about again, for pleasure as well as on public occasions, mixing more, renewing old friendships and making new ones. Among the new friends was Tony Armstrong-Jones, the young man who had taken the photographs at the Tennant-Coke wedding two years before. If he was not yet the photographic name he was to become later, he was already on his way up. Margaret's sister had seen some photographs he had taken of the children of her close friends, the Nevills, and had liked them enough to have him photograph Charles and Anne. This gave him and Margaret something to talk about when they met at a party in London.

They met again at a Halloween Ball at the Dorchester and yet again at another ball at Claridges. They joked that they always seemed to be running into each other. Margaret quickly found Tony, with his talk of photography and fashion design, actors and models, as fascinating as she had once found Peter. He told her about the photographic sets he was creating for the new John Cranko revue, *Keep Your Hair On*. He invited her to see the show and she accepted. Unfortunately, the show flopped and had already been taken off when she returned to London from Sandringham after Christmas. Instead, she included him in a party of six when she went to see the American musical, *West Side Story*. Tony, in return, invited her to a supper party at his basement flat in Pimlico. For Margaret, it was like entering a completely different world. The casual way everyone sat around, some on the floor, plates in their hands, intrigued her. Eager to copy them, to be the same, she succeeded only in spilling her food.

'I don't seem able to manage,' she said, half apologetically. 'We always have a table at home. Even for picnics.'

Tony brought her some more food and found her a folding card table to put her plate on.

So began for Margaret what was perhaps, at first, no more than a game of Christmas charades with romantic undertones. The princess became a gipsy girl in a head-scarf, an enigmatic Mata Hari in sunglasses, to visit Tony's basement flat or meet him in some quiet country town to prowl round antique shops and eat at some out-of-the-way inn. When she and Tony went to the theatre, seats were booked in the name of Gordon. Ruby Gordon was Margaret's personal maid, and there was one occasion when, switching things around, seats were booked in Margaret's name but occupied by Ruby and her husband. They were a few minutes late arriving and the manager obligingly held the curtain under the impression that he was expecting royalty that evening.

Others were likewise roped in as the game developed. Margaret would get her longtime friend Billy Wallace to escort her to socialite parties for all the world to see. But once safely inside the party venue, it was Tony, arriving separately on his motor-cycle, she danced and sat out with for most of the evening.

Delighted to see her younger daughter so alive and happy again, her widowed mother invited Tony to Royal Lodge at weekends. Taking his cue from Margaret, he would turn up in a car piled high with photographic equipment which he painstakingly unloaded and humped indoors, to create an illusion that he was there merely in a photographic capacity. And having brought so much photographic gear with him, sometimes he used it.

From time to time Margaret also saw her old love, Peter Townsend. In the aftermath of their parting Townsend had set off on a round-the-world tour to get over things. Soon after his return he called at Clarence House for a reunion with Margaret. Since then he had also been to lunch at Royal Lodge. On Townsend's side, the love he had once felt for Margaret had dimmed to affectionate friendship. The possibility of marrying her was now a thing of the past. Indeed, there was already another girl in his life, just as Tony had come into Margaret's life. The newspapers saw things differently and there was so much publicity each time Townsend met Margaret, along with a revival of old rumours, that in 1959 they decided it would be better if they met no more but pursued their separate lives and new loves.

Their last meeting, at Clarence House, was inevitably a somewhat emotional occasion. 'Oh, Peter, it's wonderful to see you,' Margaret exclaimed impulsively. He kissed her and bowed to her mother. When he left again, an hour or so later, Margaret walked hand in hand with him to the front door. He kissed her mother on both cheeks in the continental fashion; did the same to Margaret. Then, with a final wave of the hand, he was gone.

If Margaret was concerned to keep her budding romance with Tony a secret that summer, her sister also had a secret to keep. At the age of thirty-three, after a gap of nearly ten years, perhaps unexpectedly she found herself pregnant again following a tender reunion with Philip on his return from another prolonged sortie to isolated islands and outposts similar to the one which had earlier led to rumours of a marital rift. But if pregnancy was unexpected, it was nonetheless welcome, though it could hardly have come at a more inopportune time. The mother-to-be was about to embark on the longest royal tour she had undertaken since the round-the-world trip which followed her coronation. This time it was the turn of Canada, which had been omitted from the previous itinerary. Her planned schedule called for her to spend some seven weeks trekking right across Canada and back. It was hardly the sort of endurance test a pregnant woman would normally undertake, but the Queen in her – Queen of Canada as well as the United Kingdom – would not permit her to call it off.

There were times, during those weeks in Canada, when she positively glowed with the bloom of approaching motherhood. But there were also other times when

148

morning sickness and other upsets of pregnancy, on top of long-distance travel and innumerable public functions, left her strained and exhausted. She insisted on keeping her pregnancy a secret and all manner of other excuses – trouble with her teeth, sinus, something she had eaten – were trotted out by way of explanation. A leisurely return trip by sea had been planned, but by the time the tour ended she was so ill that it seemed wiser to her to fly back so that royal physicians could take a look at her. They packed her off to Balmoral to rest and recuperate.

Her pregnancy was fast approaching a point at which it could no longer be concealed. It was time to tell the children that there would soon be a small addition to the family. Which did they want, she asked them, a baby brother or a baby sister? Both plumped for a brother. It would be someone to go riding with now that Charles was away at school, explained Anne, nine that August.

Aunt Alice, in her thirties, had had a miscarriage, due, some of the family thought, to continuing to ride in pregnancy. Anxious not to make the same mistake, the Queen gave up her customary daily ride beside the Dee. Instead, she took more and longer tramps across the moors, a form of exercise she enjoyed anyhow. Charles was nearly eleven now and Philip was teaching him to shoot. There were family picnics in the hills with Papa doing the cooking on a new barbecue outfit he had picked up in Canada. The children helped out, mixing the batter for pancakes.

Anne had received a new bicycle for her birthday and rode it everywhere. One day she was too tired to ride back from a family picnic to which she had cycled. There was no room for the bicycle in the Land Rover and Philip volunteered to ride it back for her. It was a long haul over bumpy ground and his weight proved too much for Anne's small cycle. The Land Rover was out of sight when the front wheel buckled beneath him and he eventually arrived back at Balmoral after a long tramp with the bicycle on his shoulder.

To please her sister – and also perhaps to take a closer look at the new man in Margaret's life – the Queen invited Tony Armstrong-Jones to Balmoral that summer. If she took a liking to him, Philip was slightly less enthusiastic. Tony did not fit into the outdoor life of the family at play. While Philip and the rest were always up by eight and rarin' to go, Tony preferred to lie abed until ten.

'Where is the bloody man?' Philip would demand as he and others waited for Tony to show up for a shooting excursion. 'Still in bed, I suppose.' One morning, tired of waiting, he drove off without him. 'He'll have to follow under his own steam,' he snorted.

Back in London, Margaret and Tony's romantic game blossomed into courtship. They were seeing a lot of each other now, at Royal Lodge, at parties, at out of the way places and at a hideaway home Tony borrowed in London's dockland, a timbered house built by some long-dead sea captain and overhanging the Thames. It was a romantic setting for secret courtship which delighted not only Margaret but also her mother when Margaret took her there. Tony had only one room which he furnished with do-it-yourself cupboards, an electric cooker, a brass-bound chest in which he stored wine, a fishnet hammock, a rocking chair, a divan which had seen better days, and any amount of nineteenth and eighteenth century bric-à-brac.

But, for Margaret, memories of Peter Townsend, revived by his visit to Clarence House earlier that year, still lingered. Then came news of Townsend's engagement to Marie-Luce Jamagne, a young Belgian half his age with a striking resemblance to Margaret. Townsend had met her, in curious fashion, shortly after he was first 'exiled' to Brussels. It was at a horse show in which she was competing. Her horse threw her and Townsend had rushed to her aid. After that he became an increasingly frequent visitor to the Jamagne home in Antwerp and in 1958, when he repeated his round-the-world tour, though this time by air, Marie-Luce went with him.

150

The newspapers of the time had been full of stories about the couple and photographs of them, so Margaret should have been prepared. Even so, the news of their engagement came as a shock. It was a stop-press item in an evening newspaper. She read it, picked up the newspaper and threw it across the room.

Shortly afterwards, her own engagement to Tony was announced. It would have been announced earlier but for the fact that her sister was expecting a baby and it was thought better to delay things until that happy event was over.

At Christmas Tony was invited to spend a few days at Sandringham. Though there was as yet no official announcement, as far as the family were concerned he and Margaret were already engaged. Elizabeth's pregnancy was now too far advanced for her to attend the wedding of Uncle Dickie's younger daughter, Pamela, to David Hicks and Philip went on his own. As with many mothers-to-be, she developed a 'sweet tooth' in pregnancy, with a longing for things like honey and ice cream which she normally avoided as fattening. Pregnancy also set her thinking about the family name of Windsor.

As Queen, she had been young and inexperienced at the time she relinquished her husband's name of Mountbatten on the advice of Churchill and others. Now, nearly eight years later with her third child due in a few weeks, she felt that the change had been too sweeping; unfair to her husband. Her doubts were accentuated by a newspaper report she read of a sermon delivered by Dr Thomas Bloomer, Bishop of Carlisle. 'We in this country have a respect for titles,' Dr Bloomer had said, 'but a family name transcends these and stirs deeper and more powerful emotions.'

A family name . . . Windsor or Mountbatten? Which should it be? As Queen, she still wished to preserve the name of Windsor which Grandpapa England had adopted for the family long before she was born. As a wife and mother, she now wanted the children, at least, to bear their father's equally adopted name of Mountbatten. So she decided upon a compromise. As Queen, she would continue to reign as a Windsor, but the children from now on would be Mountbatten-Windsors. A royal Order in Council effected the necessary change, as it happened a bare eleven days before the baby was born.

Charles and Anne got their wish, another brother. If Philip was not completely happy about his children being Mountbatten-Windsors instead of plain Mountbattens or Windsor-Mountbattens, he was pleased with his wife's ready acceptance of Andrew, in memory of Philip's dead father, as the name of their third child and second son, with Albert, in memory of her own father, as runner-up.

As close-knit as always, other members of the family flocked to the palace to see the latest addition, Granny, Margo, Aunt Marina and her daughter Alex. Marina and Alex haggled good-naturedly, as relatives will, over whether the new baby looked more like his mother or his father. Philip was not bothered as to who the baby resembled, simply delighted to have another son. He dashed around crying 'It's a boy', opened bottles of celebratory champagne and loaded his tired, if smiling, wife with a huge bouquet of carnations and roses.

Uncle Dickie was delighted that his own family name of Mountbatten was now to be linked with the royal name of Windsor. He was in London when the baby was born, waiting to welcome his younger daughter and her new husband back from their honeymoon. Edwina was not with him. She was away again, though not on one of the harum-scarum jaunts of younger days. Since the war her boundless vitality had found new, more worthwhile outlets. Four days after Pamela's wedding she had left for the Far East to carry out a tour of inspection in her role as superintendent-in-chief of the St John's Ambulance Brigade. She was already suffering from angina and reached North Borneo so exhausted she was obliged to spend a morning in bed. She managed to get up in the afternoon, kept three appointments and went on to attend a reception in the evening. But she did not stay long.

It was three in the morning when her husband was awakened by the telphone. He answered it to learn the news that Edwina, like cousin Bertie, had died in her sleep. He sat there like a man stunned. Unpredictable though she had been, even wayward at times, she had pulled with him, supported him, won friends and influenced people on his behalf. If their marriage had not always been plain sailing, it had yet survived crises which could have wrecked lesser marriages and recent years had brought growing happiness. Now it was over and he was left with only the memories of Edwina's tremendous vitality and zest for life.

13

Wedding Bells

A bare three months after Peter Townsend married Marie-Luce Jamagne in Brussels, Margaret married Tony Armstrong-Jones in London. For all that the wedding took place in Westminster Abbey and saw the streets of London packed with rejoicing crowds, the family insisted upon regarding it as a 'private' occasion, a form of words which meant that while the bride's elder sister might meet and mingle with such assorted guests as the bridegroom's mother (divorced and re-married), his stepmother (also divorced) and his father (twice divorced and now married for the third time), officially the Monarch did not.

Private or public, it was very much a family occasion. With no father to give Margaret in marriage, her brother-in-law, Philip, filled the breach. Her niece Anne was one of eight youthful bridesmaids. Margaret's mother and sister helped to see her and Tony off on their Caribbean honeymoon with a shower of imitation rose petals. Sister Elizabeth also loaned the newlyweds her luxurious royal yacht as a means of transport.

So Margaret's traumatic love-life had an almost fairytale ending. Or so it seemed at the time, and the glamour of the event once again drew newsmen to London from all over the world. Unfortunately, one of them followed up the story of Margaret's wedding with another about her mother. The widowed Elizabeth was planning to marry again, so ran the story. She would take as her second husband her dapper, Edwardian-looking Treasurer, Sir Arthur Penn.

Following her daughter's wedding, the Queen Mother had left for a tour of what was then Northern Rhodesia. She was in Kitwe when she learned of the story about her which had been published in the New York *Daily News*. It was one of the few occasions, perhaps the only one, on which she truly lost her temper. The report was completely untrue and she said so in a few well-chosen words which had to be watered down for subsequent public consumption. Even watered down, they castigated the story as 'absolute nonsense'.

Friends of the newlyweds who prophesied that Margaret's marriage to Tony would last 'no more than two years' similarly seemed to be spouting absolute nonsense. Whatever her share of the blame for the ultimate break-up (sixteen rather than two years later), Margaret, at the outset, was a loyal, loving and devoted, if sometimes temperamental, wife. She supported Tony when he said he had no wish for a title. She sided with him in his desire to carry on working as a professional photographer and later on when he became 'artistic adviser' to the *Sunday Times*. But that was in the future and, meanwhile, Tony faced much the same problem that Philip had faced in his own early days of marriage. It is difficult to be the man of the house and pay the bills when your wife's income is so much greater than your own. The problem was overcome by Margaret transferring part of her own Civil List income to Tony's bank account each quarter. The sum had increased to £15,000 a year on marriage.

Others helped to get the marriage off to a good start. The bride's sister made a twenty-one room apartment at Kensington Palace available to them as a home and Margaret's old friend, Colin Tennant, gave them a plot of land on the remote island of Mustique. There they built the hideaway holiday home which was to make such big headlines years later when it was Roddy Llewellyn instead of Tony who went there with Margaret.

In those early days of marriage Margaret was very much in love with Tony. Or if she was not, she thought she was. She enjoyed being mistress of her own home and looked on admiringly as Tony set to work on another do-it-your-self project, a massive desk being built in solid teak. Half a mile or so away, at Buckingham Palace, Margaret's elder sister was equally happy as she settled to the fresh era of motherhood which fate had brought her way. If she could not take a complete sabbatical – the contents of her dispatch boxes continued to plague her daily – she could, and did, cut down on public functions, forego evening engagements altogether and cut out foreign travel for the first year of the baby's life. In the privacy of her palace apartment and the nursery immediately above, she devoted herself to the new baby, nursing him in her arms, playing with him, wheeling him round the garden in the high-bodied old-fashioned baby carriage treasured from the babyhoods of Charles and Anne. Philip too revelled in the excitement of being a father again, dashing up to the nursery each evening to see his infant son before going out to whatever public function he was due to attend that night.

For Margaret, married life, lacking children as yet, was very different. And very different too from the constrained, almost strait-laced royal world in which she had previously been cocooned. It was fun going out and about with Tony, meeting and mixing with actors and actresses, stage designers and choreographers, pop singers and jazz musicians, movie stars and television personalities. Yet she could never quite shake off the straightjacket of her royal background and early upbringing, never quite manage to meet such people on their own level, never quite bring herself to accept their more casual attitudes. She wanted to be one of the crowd, but she also expected deference to her royal status, bridling if she was not addressed as 'Ma'am' at least. Of course, accustomed to deference all her life, she did not see it that way. To her, it was no more than the natural order of things. By the same token, if others in the select circle which revolved around her and Tony thought that she wanted her own way too much, she did not. Nor, perhaps, did she see her attitude to her newly-acquired husband as possessive – which it was – and if Tony initially enjoyed being possessed by a real-life princess, he was later to find her attitude stifling and oppressive and react against it.

While Margaret was revelling in her first year of married life, another royal romance was running its secret course. Her cousin Eddy, the young Duke of Kent, had fallen in love with a Yorkshire lass, the daughter of the Lord Lieutenant of the North Riding, Katharine Worsley, a blue-eyed blonde whose appearance of porcelain fragility went well with the Dresden-style shepherdess dress she wore to the fancy dress ball at which they first met. After that, as with Margaret and Tony, they seemed to be constantly running into each other while Eddy was stationed at Catterick with his regiment, at cocktail parties and dances, at point to point meetings and village cricket matches. That something like four years were to lapse between that first meeting and ultimate marriage was not due to any lack of ardour on Eddy's part. Reserved though he still was, he was no longer the almost painfully shy young man he had been when he first joined the army. The delay was due to the sort of problems which seem to beset all royal romances. On the one hand there was his mother, the widowed Marina, a Royal of the old school for all the comparative informality of her exiled upbringing, hopeful that her elder son might marry a princess as she herself had married a prince. On the other hand there was Kate herself, hesitant – like the Queen Mother before her – about embarking on the more rigid way of life which must be her lot if she married into the Royal Family. If Eddy was not the son of a King, as Bertie had been, he was cousin to the Queen and the pressures of public life would be considerable.

No royal romance can be kept totally secret and inevitably there were rumours which found their way into the newspapers. Rumours were followed by the equally inevitable denials. No, Katharine had not been to Germany to visit him while he was stationed there with the Royal Scots Greys. That particular denial was true as far as it went. In fact they had met in the Tyrol while Eddy was on leave from his regiment. So anxious was he to cover his romantic trail that he went there without booking out from his camp . . . and was duly reprimanded on his return.

The Queen became privy to the secret when Eddy slipped away from the Sandringham family party immediately after Christmas in order to see the New Year in with Katharine at her home in Yorkshire. Soon afterwards, Katharine went to Canada to stay with her brother and his wife. She needed time to think. By the time she returned her mind was made up. Obtaining the Queen's formal permission to marry, as Eddy was bound to do under the same Royal Marriages Act which had contributed towards Margaret's parting from Peter Townsend, was scarcely more than a formality and by the time their betrothal was officially announced they had, in fact, already been secretly engaged for some weeks.

With the exception of Wallis Warfield, brides of the previous generation, Elizabeth, Marina and Alice, had all been obliged to make the trek to London when they married into Grandpapa England's family. But times and attitudes had changed, and for his wedding in the summer of 1961, Eddy journeyed north to marry on the bride's patch, if not exactly in the church in the village where she lived, at least in nearby York Minster.

Still aggrieved that Wallis had not been granted the status of Royal Highness, David turned down an invitation to Eddy's wedding, just as he had earlier declined to be present at Margaret's. Another invited guest missing from the wedding was Frances, the wife of Viscount Althorp, later Earl Spencer, though not out of pique. She was unable to attend because of pregnancy, though the younger of her two daughters, Jane, attended on Katharine as one of her bridesmaids.

Frances herself was the daughter of that Baron Fermoy who had been such a close friend of Bertie's. Her mother Ruth was a close friend of Bertie's widow, as well as being one of her ladies-in-waiting. The family had, in fact, been near neighbours of the Royals at Sandringham since the 1930s when Lord Fermoy, whose Irish peerage did not debar him from sitting in the Commons, was Member of Parliament for the district. And it was at Sandringham, in Park House on 1 July 1961, that Frances gave birth to her third daughter.

Charles was twelve, rising thirteen, at the time, a schoolboy at Cheam still, all of which did not prevent various women's magazines from speculating as to who he might one day marry. Princess Anne-Marie of Denmark, later to marry Constantine of Greece, topped most of the lists. No one, of course, gave any thought to the newborn babe at Park House, christened Diana Frances in the church of St Mary Magdalene which the Royals attend each Sunday whenever they are at Sandringham.

Reluctant though she may have been to leave a house so full of memories, the widowed Marina, with her daughter Alex, now made her Kensington Palace apartment her home, leaving Coppins vacant for her son and his new bride. Financially hard-pressed as the family had been ever since George's wartime death, Eddy found himself having to face the fact that the place needed a lot doing to it if it was to be restored to what it had been in his father's day. The summer house in the garden was in danger of collapsing and the swimming pool was full of weeds. He re-built the one and cleaned out the other. With help from the bride's father, they had the kitchen modernised and splashed out on new carpets and curtains. A portable television set, one of their wedding gifts, augmented the ancient console with its small twelve-inch screen which had been there since pre-war days. But some things remained unchanged. Portraits of the dead George and his widow stayed in place and George's last note, 'Please do not move anything on this desk', written two days before he died, was carefully preserved still, as it had been throughout the nearly twenty years of Marina's widowhood.

For Margaret, marriage had quickly followed its natural course and she too was pregnant by the time Eddy married. This caused a slight problem for her sister, a problem harking back to Grandpapa England's day. While taking steps to ensure that his sons' children were born with titles, he had not done so for children born to his daughter. But at least they had had the minor titles stemming from the Harewood earldom to fall back on. Margaret's child, similarly omitted when Bertie had assured titles for the children of his elder daughter, would have no such titular cushion. Unless something was done about it, the babe would be born merely Master or Miss Armstrong-Jones. The Queen wanted something better than that for her nephew or niece and again raised the question of giving brother-in-law Tony a title. This time he accepted, while letting it be known among his friends and business associates that 'Tony Snowdon' would suffice as a democratic compromise between his old name and his new Earl of Snowdon title.

As a result, Margaret's first child, a boy, entered the world not as David Armstrong-Jones, but as Viscount Linley, while a sister to be born a few years later would have the matching designation of Lady Sarah Armstrong-Jones. There was no such problem of a title for the son born to Eddy's wife, Katharine, the new Duchess of Kent. Because Eddy was Duke of Kent, his son automatically qualified for the subsidiary title of Earl of St

Andrews. They named him George, after Eddy's dead father.

Philip was no longer the frustrated and sometimes depressed man he had been in the early days of his wife's monarchy. Around his nebulous role of Consort he had constructed a busy life of his own. He was always on the go, it seemed, always dashing off somewhere. Home from school one day, Charles asked if Papa would be in for lunch. 'If he takes on much more, he soon won't be in for breakfast,' sighed the boy's mother.

She was on her own at Windsor, with Philip away in South America, when a telephone call from Cheam informed her that Charles had acute appendicitis. Sir Wilfrid Sheldon, the royal pediatrician who had been called into consultation by the school doctor, advised an immediate operation. She gave her consent.

An ambulance made a midnight dash from Cheam to the Great Ormond Street children's hospital in London where Charles was operated on in the early hours of the morning. He was doing nicely, the Queen was told, and she sent off a cable to Philip in Venezuela. With Charles out of danger, there seemed no reason for his father to cut short his South American tour, but a telephone was installed in the boy's room at the hospital so that the two of them could have a long-distance father-and-son chat. The Queen drove to the hospital to visit her son, taking along the customary get-well offerings of flowers and fruit. However, Charles was not up to eating the fruit; he was still on a liquid diet. There were other cheering visits for the young invalid from Granny, Aunt Margo and sister Anne. Andrew, now two, was also taken along to see his big brother.

Charles was now thirteen, time to transfer from Cheam to Gordonstoun, another of Papa's old schools. He liked Gordonstoun no more than he had liked Cheam, though perhaps for different reasons which he himself was too young to understand. He felt the need to live up to his father's more extrovert schoolboy image, but was not himself – as yet, at least – the sort of youngster his father had been. What he did know was that he was not happy and he took advantage of a visit to Granny, one weekend when she was in Scotland, to plead with her to help him. But sorry as she may have felt for her small grandson, the Queen Mother was too wise a mother-in-law to interfere in something so dear to Philip's heart as shaping his son in his own image. Instead, she told the boy he must stick it out. 'There are times in life when we all have to do things we don't like,' she said, perhaps with memories of the abdication and its aftermath.

Another summer, another family wedding. This time the bride was Eddy's sister, Alex, tall and Junoesque, with the same fascinating 'trout's eyes' as her mother. The bridegroom was the Hon. Angus Ogilvy, younger son of the Earl of Airlie, a birthright which had not prevented him from carving out his own career in the world of big business. And marriage into the Royal Family, he made it diplomatically plain from the outset, would not be permitted to interfere with his workaday life. For him, there was to be no retreat into the private world of Buckingham Palace, as Tony had done ahead of marriage to Margaret. Instead, he went back and forth to his office in London's Old Broad Street very much as usual. Even the day before the wedding, which was also the morning after a ball at Windsor Castle which did not end until four a.m., he was up again after no more than four hours' sleep and at work as usual. For Angus, there was to be no trekking around at his wife's heels on public occasions, as Tony did in the early days of marriage to Margaret. Alex could carry on with royal chores by all means, but she must not expect her husband to be a mere royal remittance man. Neither was there any question of a title for him, then or later. As a result, the couple's children, for all that their mother is a princess, were to be born simply James and Marina Ogilvy. It was all, perhaps because Alex was a very different type of young woman from Margaret, to work out surprisingly well.

As usual, others of the family rallied round to give the couple a good send-off. The Queen paid the bills for the pre-wedding reception and ball at which 1,600 guests danced to two bands. For Charles, now fourteen, and Anne, twelve, it was their first really grown-up occasion. Charles danced with Granny and Anne with Angus. After all, she was again chief bridesmaid, as she had been for Katharine's wedding at York Minster. Philip took a whole host of European royals and near-royals who came over for the wedding on a magical mystery coach tour of the countryside around London with a pub lunch thrown in for good measure. Eddy and Katharine flew home from Hong Kong, where Eddy's regiment was then stationed, so that he could deputise for his dead father and give his sister in marriage. And the 'something old' which Alex wore for her wedding was the same tiara her mother had worn when she married a king's son nearly thirty years before.

Ever since Charles went off to boarding school, Anne had been badgering her parents to be allowed to follow suit. She was not in the least put off by the fact that her brother did not like school. Philip saw no reason why she should not go, but left the decision to her mother. Finally mother said yes and Anne, hair trimmed to comply with school regulations, went to Benenden. More extrovert, more self-confident and more competitive than her elder brother at that time, she settled down quickly and easily to schoolgirl life. As Charles had done at Cheam, she found herself doing the sort of chores which had automatically been done for her at the palace, washing her own undies, sweeping out the dormitory and waiting on table at mealtimes. Only one thing initially baffled her: she had no idea how to make her own bed, she confessed. One of the other girls in the same dormitory showed her how it was done. Just as her mother's conversation, during her time in the ATS, had been sprinkled with references to sparking plugs and sprockets, so Anne's conversation, when she was home on vacation, was suddenly sprinkled with schoolgirl slang. 'Greased rats', her parents were amused to learn, were iced buns and 'Ganges mud' was chocolate pudding. 'Dead man's leg' was baked jam roll.

Of the children, only Andrew, a sturdy and impish three-year-old who reminded Philip's mother very much of what Philip himself had been like in childhood, was now at home. Not that there was any danger of him being brought up as virtually an only child. His mother, to her delight, was again pregnant.

14

Worry and Sadness

For almost a century, with rare exceptions and a few omissions, the family had gathered together at Sandringham each year for what the absentee David once described as 'a Dickensian Christmas in a Cartier setting'. It started in the days when Edward VII was a young Prince of Wales, though he preferred a house party of friends to relatives. Especially friends with attractive wives. It became a true family party in the days of Grandpapa England, to whom Sandringham meant so much. David would almost certainly have put a stop to it had he stayed on the throne. But he didn't, and his brother Bertie, as sentimentally attached to Sandringham as his father before him, continued the tradition. Elizabeth II, if slightly less attached to the place than her father and grandfather had been, carried on . . . until 1963.

For a variety of reasons, that year was to see the end of the Sandringham Christmas tradition. One of the reasons was the growing size of the family. Large and sprawling though the 'Big House' might be, it could no longer conveniently accommodate the growing regiment of children and all their attendant staff, nannies, nursemaids, nursery footmen and suchlike. Four of the wives – the Queen herself, Margaret, cousin Alex and sister-in-law Katharine – were all in varying stages of expectancy that Christmas of 1963.

Christmas Day was also Alex's birthday. She was twenty-eight, and the most advanced in pregnancy of the four. It was her first child, and a son, James, was born at the end of February. Indeed, but for the fact that 1964 was a leap year he would not have been born until 1 March. As it was, he came into the world on 29 February.

Other babies followed at the rate of one a month to swell the ever-growing ranks of the family until Grandpapa England's descendants, including the Lascelles grandchildren of his daughter Mary, totalled a baker's dozen in the fourth generation alone . . . with yet more to come in the future. The Queen had her fourth child, Edward, on 10 March; Eddy's wife gave birth to her second, a daughter Helen, on 28 April; while Margaret had her second, also a daughter, Sarah, on 1 May.

As a bride-to-be the Queen had once said that she hoped for a family of four children. Now, after more than sixteen years of marriage, that courtship dream had finally come true, even if one of the two girls she had hoped for had turned out to be yet another boy. Four children of very different character virtually from birth: Charles quiet and contented as a baby, shy and unsure in boyhood; Anne something of a problem child; Andrew a confident, demanding reincarnation of his father; and now Edward – 'the quietest of all my children', the Queen told her friends.

Not all the members of the extended family were disappointed by the decision to switch from Sandringham to Windsor for future family Christmases. Marina had long wearied of trekking all the way to Norfolk, while for Charles and Anne, now in their teens, spending Christmas at Windsor meant that they could more conveniently attend parties given by their friends. Christmas at Windsor, the first year of the changeover, also enabled them to give their own dance for their teenage friends, over a hundred of them, with a sprinkling of grown-ups – the royal parents, Granny and Aunt Margo, Marina and Alex

– to keep a benevolent eye on things. The Twist was all the rage that year and Anne danced her feet off. At first Charles was rather slower to join in. 'Why don't you ask someone to dance?' his grandmother encouraged him. 'I'm watching out for the prettiest girl,' her sixteen-year-old grandson informed her.

However, there was not to be a complete break with the old Sandringham tradition. If a Christmas gathering of the whole family was no longer practical, at least the Queen and those of her immediate family could go there immediately after Christmas, in time for New Year and the ancient 'first footing' ceremony, another family tradition. On the stroke of midnight the front door was opened to admit a tall, dark 'stranger' – the part of the 'stranger' being played by the tallest and darkest of the royal footmen – bearing symbolic gifts, a potted plant and a lump of polished coal.

While a fresh generation of babies was swelling the ranks of the family at one end of the scale, at the other end the years were also taking their toll of or leaving their mark on those of the older generation. The 'exiled' David was no longer the dashing, rebellious prince of the Roaring Twenties, but aged and ailing, and early in 1965 he returned briefly to Britain to enter the London Clinic for eye surgery. Wallis travelled with him.

Their arrival in London found David's niece, the Queen, again trapped between the conflicting demands of family loyalty and constitutional necessity as she had been in the matter of her sister's attachment to Peter Townsend. As Queen, she was still not prepared to do for her uncle what her father had deemed it wiser to leave undone. As David's niece, she felt sorry that the evening of his life – he was turned seventy now – should still find him cut off from the rest of the family. In an attempt to heal the rift, she twice went to the Clinic to visit him. She saw Wallis at the same time, the first occasion on which they had met since Wallis was still Mrs Simpson and the

Queen a girl of ten. Marina, for all that she had so obstinately refused to visit David and Wallis when they were on honeymoon, also felt that the past was best forgotten and called in at the Clinic to see her Windsor in-laws. David's sister, Mary, a widow now for nearly twenty years, also paid them a visit. But there was no visit from Bertie's widow.

As things turned out, it proved to be the last time David was ever to see his sister. Within a fortnight of visiting him in the London Clinic she herself was dead from a heart attack.

By now it had at last begun to dawn on Philip that his eldest son was not altogether happy at Gordonstoun, however much he himself may have enjoyed schoolboy life there a generation before. Of course, it had been a very different school in those days, smaller, more close-knit and companionable. In any event, Charles was by no means the sort of boy his father had been. The problem was how to resolve the situation without doing something which might come across as an unfortunate reflection on Gordonstoun.

By happy coincidence, Sir Robert Menzies was over from Australia at the time. A chat with him when he visited the Queen at Balmoral pointed to a possible way out. An exchange spell at a school in the Commonwealth would give Charles a much-needed break from Gordonstoun without investing the move with any critical undertones. Sir Robert suggested an isolated Australian education outpost called Timbertop, a branch of the Geelong Church of England Grammar School.

It seemed an excellent stop-gap measure, but what of the future? Because the Queen's family is also the Royal Family, because the eldest son was, and is, heir to the throne, his future training was too important to be left to his parents alone. Others must have a finger in the pie. So a planning conference to take decisions on Charles's future was convened at Buckingham Palace.

Charles himself, though the person most affected by whatever might be decided, was not there. His mother was, but merely looked on and listened. Deferring as always to her husband in matters of family, she let him do the talking for both of them. 'Send the boy to sea,' Uncle Dickie advocated. Old seadog that he was, he still saw a spell at sea, as he had told Bertie all those years before, as the best possible training for kingship. Dartmouth and then the Royal Navy, that was it. Someone pointed out that George VI had also gone to university. Shouldn't Charles do the same? Good idea. But which university? It was left for the boy's parents to decide this. Neither knew very much about universities and they were finally content to settle for Trinity College, Cambridge, which Charles's dead grandfather had gone to nearly half a century before.

First there was to be Timbertop.

For all that Australia was a totally different environment and the boys at Timbertop a very different, more down to earth breed, Charles settled down there much more quickly and easily than he had ever done at Gordonstoun, and his stay there was to mark the start of a remarkable metamorphosis in his character. From being a nervous, uncertain, almost painfully shy youngster, very much like the dead Bertie before him, he gradually became more outgoing, more confident and sure of himself. It did not happen all at once, of course, and it did not all happen at Timbertop. Trinity and the Royal Navy, in the years to come, were to make their contribution to the enormous change in his character. But Timbertop saw the beginning of the metamorphosis. His Aunt Margo, with her insistence that even close friends should address her as 'Ma'am', at least in front of others, would have been horrified to hear her nephew termed 'you pommy bastard' by his new schoolmates down under. Charles thought it a huge joke and took it in the right spirit. For the first time in his schoolboy life he found himself mixing with other youngsters who treated him as an equal, not as a prince, and something in his psychological make-up responded to it. Little by little he began to emerge from the protective cocoon he had woven around himself at Cheam and Gordonstoun, and his grandmother, on a tour of Australia, was surprised and delighted by the change in him when she re-arranged her tour schedule somewhat in order to meet up with him. There were no tears this time, no turning to Granny for comfort, no plea to intercede with his parents. On the contrary, she was pleased to hear that he was enjoying Australian school life so much that he had already telephoned his parents in London to ask if he could stay on longer.

Philip, meeting up with his son at the 1966 Commonwealth Games in Jamaica, also remarked on the change in him and was delighted by it. No longer was he a boy crawling unwilling to school, drooping around with hunched shoulders and downcast eyes, but an assured and sturdy youngster striding around with shoulders braced well back and a sometimes over-hearty bone-crushing handshake copied from the Aussies with whom he had been mixing.

Another Christmas . . . and a worrying gap in the family gathering at Windsor. After a long spell of robust good health interrupted only by the need for an appendectomy three years previously, Granny was in hospital. When she went in for a check-up, tests had revealed a partial obstruction necessitating surgery. The good news was that she was well on the road to recovery and, though she could not make it to Windsor for Christmas, she was sufficiently restored to health soon after to join her elder daughter and her grandchildren at Sandringham.

On Philip's side of the family too there were health worries. Letters from his sisters in Germany told of his mother's failing health. She was in her eighties, fifteen years older than her brother Dickie, almost of a different generation.

For all that he was the product of a broken home, his parents separating not long after they were exiled from Greece, his father heading for the pleasures of Monte Carlo while his mother went to live with her daughters in Germany and later back to Greece, Philip was always a loyal and dutiful son. As a schoolboy, he wrote regularly to the father he so seldom saw, enclosing snapshots from time to time to show how he was coming along. His father had died in 1944 and after the war Philip went to Monte Carlo to wind up his affairs. They were few enough. Philip inherited only a signet ring, a few suits and his father's old shaving brush. He had the brush re-bristled and used it himself. With the end of the war, his mother had left Greece again to live with her daughters in Germany. Since then, she had visited London several times, staying with her son and daughter-in-law at their palace home. Between such visits Philip would fly out to Germany to see her from time to time. Uncle Dickie flew with him on one occasion, his sister's seventieth birthday. Charles and Anne had been with their father too on several occasions to visit their other, older grandmother. But, for years, Philip had been unable to take his wife along.

It was not her fault; not that she did not want to go. Yet just as she was barred from inviting Philip's sisters to her wedding, so for years, because she was Queen, because Germany was the old enemy, she was not permitted to visit either them or her mother-in-law. Not until she and Philip had been married nearly eighteen years was the ban lifted, and only then because the government of the day felt that a state visit to Germany might be diplomatically advantageous. However, Philip took advantage of the occasion to arrange a couple of family gatherings with his mother, sisters, brothers-in-law and a whole horde of nieces and nephews. He also took his wife to see the school at Salem at which he had spent a year of his boyhood. The desk he had sat in over thirty years before was still there, with his initial carved on it.

Now, with news of his mother's illness, he again flew out to Germany to see her. Worried by how he found her, nothing would satisfy him but he must bring her back to Britain with him and arrange for her admission to a hospital in London. Nor, when she was well enough to leave hospital, would he hear of her returning to Germany. Instead, he arranged with his wife that his mother should have her own small apartment at the palace.

There were problems too at this time with Anne. Her schooldays were over and she had no wish to go to university, as Charles had done. All she wanted to do was ride horses. 'It is the one thing I do well and can be seen to do well,' she argued. She was to get her way later, but not at this time. Her parents felt she had to do something to justify her official allowance. Initially, she enjoyed the succession of minor engagements which came her way, bringing a teenage verve to the solemnity of public occasions. She was constantly doing the unexpected, driving a double-decker bus on one occasion, an army tank on another, firing a sub-machine gun from the hip with all the aplomb of a girl in a James Bond movie, and was briefly the darling of the press. But the novelty soon wore off and she resented the constant attentions of reporters and photographers. In Britain, because of the aura surrounding even a teenage princess, she could get away with displaying her resentment more or less openly. But overseas, in countries where people are less willing to genuflect to royalty, she could not and a growing stream of criticism flowed in her wake.

There were also problems in her personal life. Once away from school, she was cut off from the mainstream of teenage life. She had few, if any, friends – not even a sister to keep her company, as her mother had had at the same age – and, at a time when she was going through the change from girlhood to womanhood, hardly any opportunity of meeting boys of her own age. She became moody and depressed, and her parents were worried

172

about her. It was, curiously, her father who realised what was wrong and set about putting things right. He had a quiet word with some of his sailing and polo-playing cronies who had offspring of about the same age as Anne, with the result that she became one of a swinging set of bright young things, going to discos, nightclubs and theatres, even dancing on stage at a performance of *Hair* which she attended one evening. Anne was not really cut out to be a swinger, though she projected the image for a time, any more than she was cut out for a life of public chores. Horses were still the big love of her life and a riding career her ambition for the future.

Since her meetings with Uncle David and Wallis at the London Clinic, the Queen had been more anxious than ever to heal the split which had divided the family all these years. The opportunity came with the unveiling of a plaque at Marlborough House to the memory of Queen Mary, her grandmother and David's mother. What more fitting than to invite him and his wife to attend. The question was: would they accept? He had been invited to Margaret's wedding, and Eddy's, but had declined to attend either because of what he had still regarded as the slight on Wallis. However, his niece sensed that age and failing health had mellowed his earlier bitterness. So she invited him and Wallis and, this time, they accepted. They arrived by boat at Southampton on their way back to Paris from New York. David's cousin and close friend, Dickie Mountbatten, met them off the boat and took them with him to Broadlands, his country home. In London, the Queen placed one of her royal cars at their disposal and later laid on a royal aircraft to take them on to Paris. As far as she was concerned, the past was past and best forgotten. But her mother still could not bring herself to unbend more than to accept a peck on the cheek from David with a handshake sufficing for Wallis.

Of the five children of Grandpapa England who had survived into maturity, three – Bertie, George and Mary

– were now dead. David was ailing, and so was Harry. He had not been in consistent good health since 1965. He had been driving back to his home at Barnwell after attending Churchill's funeral when his car inexplicably went off the road. A party of Mansfield miners on a day's outing came to the rescue and Harry, Alice and their chauffeur (in the back of the car at the time of the accident) were taken to hospital. Alice had broken an arm and her nose and the chauffeur had damaged his ribs. Harry was suffering from no more than shock, but worried that a slight stroke might perhaps have been the cause of the accident.

Shortly afterwards, touring Australia, there was no doubt that he had had a stroke. He collapsed in Government House just as he was due to attend the Anzac Day parade in Canberra. Alice and his valet helped him to his feet. He rested a few minutes, took a stroll in the garden and insisted upon attending the parade as though nothing had happened. The following January, almost on the eve of leaving for Malaysia, he suddenly seemed to lose track of things. A doctor was called, but he rallied and, as in Australia, insisted on going ahead. He was still shaky and slow-thinking when he arrived in Singapore, but seemed to pick up as the tour progressed. The tour over, he and Alice enjoyed a restful holiday in Jamaica. On their way back, they met David during a stopover in New York. It was the last time the two brothers were to see each other.

In May 1967, he had two more strokes in quick succession. This time there could be no question of carrying on with business as usual. His speech was affected and his body paralysed to an extent which saw him confined to a wheelchair.

William, his elder son, the wartime baby born when Alice was approaching forty, was now in his twenties. Along with his younger brother, Richard, he had early determined not to make the Royal Family into which he had been born a way of life. Instead, after gaining a degree in economics at Stanford University in California, he had gone into the diplomatic service, while his brother was in the process of qualifying as an architect after a spell at Magdalene College, Cambridge. It was at Cambridge, over a pot of tea and a plate of muffins at an afternoon party, that Richard met the young Danish girl he was destined to marry. He was a one-girl man. William, by contrast, found it fun to play the field. More dashing and extrovert than his younger brother, he was constantly in the news on account of his youthful adventures, romantic and otherwise. Apart from girls, flying was the great love of his life. Posted to the British embassy in Tokyo, he flew out to Japan in his own small aircraft. With his father now paralysed and confined to a wheelchair, he decided to resign from the diplomatic corps and return home to run the family estate.

It was a time of life when it must have seemed to the Queen that family worries, like London buses, never come singly but all together. Illness in the older generation and teenage problems among the younger were followed by a marital upset in the third generation. At the centre of this latest worry was her cousin George, the elder of the two sons of her dead Aunt Mary and Earl of Harewood since the death of 'Lucky' in 1947. Shortly after his father's death George had married Marion Stein, by whom he had fathered three sons in the first six years of marriage. Then in 1964 he had become a father yet again, another son, but this time his wife was not the mother. The mother of George's fourth son was his secretary, Patricia Tuckwell, a divorced Australian.

Until now, the liaison had been kept reasonably discreet so as not to distress George's mother more than was absolutely necessary, though she knew how things stood. Following his mother's death, however, he had started living openly with Patricia. Not unnaturally, his wife sued for divorce and subsequently married Jeremy Thorpe, former leader of the Liberal Party.

The divorce had not concerned his cousin in her role as

Queen. But now she was involved. George wanted to marry Patricia Tuckwell and for this, as a descendant of George II and in line of succession to the throne, however distant, he needed his cousin's formal consent under the Royal Marriage Act. Not only was the Queen now involved, but she once again found herself in the sort of family-monarchy dilemma which had confronted her at the time her sister wanted to marry Peter Townsend. If she had been unable to consent to her sister marrying a man who was the innocent party in a divorce action, how much less could she permit her cousin, divorced by his wife for adultery, to re-marry. Fortunately, it was not the unbending Churchill to whom she had to turn for advice in this latest dilemma, but the more pragmatic Harold Wilson. He lifted the burden from her shoulders by raising the matter at a Cabinet meeting and then, as prime minister, formally advising her to give consent to her cousin's re-marriage. The question thus, subtly, became a political rather than a religious one, with Elizabeth, as Queen, duty-bound to accept her prime minister's advice. She heaved a sigh of relief and gave her consent.

But the train of upset and disaster which had dogged the extended family for the past few years was not yet over. In the August of 1968 Marina, ageing now but still elegant in old age, invited her son-in-law and daughter, Angus and Alex, to lunch at Kensington Palace. It was the anniversary of her husband's fatal crash, but time had dimmed memory and it was a happy occasion. Next morning, however, she complained of feeling tired. Too tired to get up. She stayed in bed and drifted off to sleep again. Imperceptibly, sleep merged into coma and she died next day from a brain tumour without regaining consciousness. In accordance with a wish expressed long ago, her husband's body was brought from the vault at Windsor and they were buried together in the royal cemetery at Frogmore.

So death took its toll of the family . . . again and again.

By Christmas Philip's mother was too weak to accompany the rest of the family when they went to Windsor, which had now replaced Sandringham as the venue for the annual get-together. So on Christmas day son and daughter-in-law climbed into a car and drove back to London to take her her gifts and have tea with her. She did not live quite long enough to see another Christmas, though long enough to mourn for her daughter, Philip's sister Theodora, who died earlier that same year of cancer in Germany.

Amidst all this catalogue of grief and worry, there appeared, suddenly, a single bright spot. Anne, all at once, was brighter, happier, less of a worry than she had been in a long time. She had fallen in love.

15

Anne In Love

Like her mother before her, Anne was still in her teens when she first met the man she was eventually to marry. Her mother had been a mere child of thirteen when her eyes first lighted on Philip. Anne was slightly older, seventeen, when she met Mark Phillips at a dinner party to which she was invited while attending the Eridge horse trials. He was nineteen at the time, a cadet at the Royal Military College, Sandhurst, a tall, erect young man with a crinkle-faced smile, not unlike Anne's father when younger. If it was not exactly a case of love at first sight, as it had been for the Queen, there was sufficient attraction for Anne to single him out when they met again at a reception given for Britain's 1968 Olympic equestrian team in which he was reserve rider. On each occasion he greeted her with a small bow of the head, a courtly acknowledgement of her royal status which he was to continue right up to the day he eventually proposed to her.

By now, Charles was fast maturing into an immensely likeable young man, still less confident perhaps than he looked but now able to hide inherited shyness behind a mask of good humour. A spell at Trinity College, Cambridge, had continued the metamorphosis begun at Timbertop, opening a fresh window on the world. Brought up to have almost no contact with the opposite sex, apart from his teasing, extrovert sister, he was almost terrified of girls when he first arrived at Trinity. They still disturbed him when he left, but in a different way, and throughout his twenties he was to switch his affection from girl to girl as though determined to make up for lost time. Shy as he still was inwardly, he was often attracted to the brasher, more sexy type of girl and was not always as circumspect as he might have been in his choice of female companions.

In all other respects, he was an ideal son, devoted to his mother, admiring his father, especially close to Granny who saw him almost as a reincarnation of his dead grandfather, Bertie. Uncle Dickie, who had served as a substitute father to Philip in youth, became more and more a substitute grandfather to Charles. They were often together, a shared enthusiasm for the sea, polo and the bonds of family bridging the age gap. The bonds of family equally became an incentive to Charles to mend the rift which had for so long come between him and another of his great-uncles, the exiled David. Others of his generation of the family felt the same way, the same regret that an uncle who had briefly been King before they were born should live out the evening of his life in exiled isolation. For all that their mother had once ostracised David by refusing to call on him and his wife on honeymoon, both Eddy and his sister Alex went out of their way to visit him in Paris. So did their cousin William, now running the Barnwell Manor estate for his paralysed father.

Charles similarly seized upon the opportunity of an official visit to France, representing his mother at a memorial service to General de Gaulle, to make a private call upon his great-uncle. He had not long been installed as Prince of Wales with the same sort of ceremony David had undergone some six decades earlier as a boy of sixteen. So the youthful great-nephew and the ageing great-uncle had much to talk about.

Charles was increasingly turning into a chip off the old

block, the sort of son his father had always wanted him to be. In time out from his studies at Trinity he had learned to fly and, in 1971, in pursuit of the princely training programme mapped out for him earlier, he served briefly in the Royal Air Force, majoring on jets and winning his 'wings'. Philip could not have been more delighted. Attending his son's passing out parade, he was affable even to the ever-present photographers, a sect he normally regards with a somewhat jaundiced eye. Would he mind adopting a handshake pose with his son? 'I'll stand on my head if you want me to,' he quipped.

He was in a quipping mood too at the European Eventing Championship at Burghley, concealing his true feelings of fatherly pride behind a joking remark. 'I'm only here for the beer.' If Burghley was an occasion for fatherly pride on Philip's part, it was equally an occasion for motherly joy in his royal wife. Against all the odds, their sometimes temperamental daughter won the championship.

Anne had been in hospital only a short time before for the removal of an ovarian cyst. Because she was thought to be unfit after hospitalisation, and certainly out of practice, she was not included in the team which Britain entered for the championship. She took non-inclusion as a challenge and responded to it. As the royal yacht carried the family north that year for the annual vacation at Balmoral, she played endless games of deck tennis to harden her hands, which had gone soft in hospital. Leg muscles had likewise turned to flab. At Balmoral, she set about strengthening them by jogging up and down the heather-clad Scottish hills. Satisfied that she was in good physical shape again, she sent in an individual entry for the championship.

Mum, dad and others of the family were there to cheer her on. At the end of the first day's dressage, competing against the pick of riders from France, Italy, Ireland and Russia as well as Britain, she was in the lead. But only

180

just. It was a situation she had been in twice before that year, only to find victory snatched from her grasp in the later stages. At Badminton, competing for the first time in a three-day event, she had led at the end of the first day but finished only fifth. At Eridge she had again led on the first day but finished twelfth. The winner on each occasion had been Mark, now a young lieutenant in the Queen's Dragoon Guards.

The attraction she already felt for Mark perhaps acted as a personal spur. Certainly, she was resolved to prove the British selectors wrong. Determined to hang on to her slender lead, she took chances in the cross-country section. Luck was with her. A couple of risky short cuts, which might easily have ended in disaster, came off for her and a clear round in the show jumping cemented her victory. Mark trailed in sixth place.

She and Mark continued to run into each other at the various horse trials in which they both competed and at the social occasions associated with them. At Crookham, the following year, there was the customary dance at Bagshott Hall. Michael and Sally Bullen invited Anne to join their party for the occasion and she accepted. To make up their number, which included two other bachelor girls, the Bullens invited along three unattached young men. To her delight, Anne found that Mark was her escort for the evening. It was the nearest she had ever come to a blind date – or perhaps the Bullens were giving Cupid a helping hand. Either way, Anne and Mark were almost inseparable that evening.

As love blossomed between them, an older and more historic love story was drawing to its end. At his home in Paris Uncle David was dying.

As his life moved towards its close, his royal niece made another gesture towards healing the ancient rift which had split the family for so long. As her eldest son had done before her, she took time out from a state visit to France to call on her ageing uncle at his home in the Bois de Boulogne. Philip went with her. Wallis greeted them at the door and led the way upstairs to where David lay dying of cancer in a room dominated by his royal coat-of-arms.

It was the first time the Queen had ever visited her uncle in his own home . . . and the last. Eight days later David was dead. He died without ever once regretting that he had sacrificed a throne for love of Wallis, but bitter still at what had followed. Bitter that he had not been given the worthwhile job for Britain he had always wanted; bitter that the woman he took as wife had never been granted the same royal status as his sisters-in-law.

His body was brought home for burial in the family vault at Windsor. Wallis was too grief-stricken to travel with it, but followed in an aircraft which the Queen placed at her disposal. At a memorial service in St George's Chapel, Windsor, she sat between the Queen and Philip, staying overnight at Buckingham Palace, the first time she had been there since those long-ago days when David was briefly King Edward VIII and hopeful of making her Queen.

Of the five sons of Grandpapa England, only Harry now survived, imprisoned in his wheelchair at Barnwell Manor. He was to linger on for another two years. Because of his father's illness, Richard, the younger of Harry's two sons, opted for a quiet wedding when he was married that July to the young Danish girl he had been courting discreetly since they first met at Cambridge. Birgitte Eva Van Deurs was the daughter of a Danish lawyer named Aager Henriksen, but had taken her mother's maiden name when her parents separated. At the time she and Richard first met she had been at Cambridge to brush up on her English. Later, to facilitate courtship after working for a spell in Copenhagen, she had returned to Britain, securing a secretarial post at the Danish Embassy.

The wedding took place in the Norman church at

Barnwell. Harry was too ill to make even that short journey and, because of the family's wish for a quiet wedding, Elizabeth and Philip did not attend. Even without them, but with Charles, Aunt Margo, Granny and Michael of Kent among the guests, a crowd of some two thousand people braved the pouring rain to besiege the church. Compared to the pomp and circumstance with which Alex had been married at Westminster Abbey and her brother in York Minster, the actual ceremony was simplicity itself. There were no bridesmaids or boyish pages and, in a concession to the bride's Danish sense of independence, the promise to obey was omitted from her bridal vows.

The couple set up home in a modest terrace house in Camden Town from where Richard rode to work each day on a motor-cycle, signing his architectural designs 'Richard Gloucester'. Within weeks the simple note on which their marriage started was to undergo a radical change. It changed when Richard's elder brother William, best man at the wedding, died suddenly and violently at the youthful age of thirty.

It was William's enthusiasm for flying which brought about his death. The previous year he had taken part in the King's Cup air race, finishing seventh. Only six weeks after Richard's marriage, he took part in another race, the Goodyear International. He crashed while taking off from Halfpenny Green, near Wolverhampton, in his Piper Cherokee. He retracted his under-carriage and went into a tight turn away from another machine which had taken off with him. It was all over in seconds. He skimmed the roof of a nearby house, clipped the top of a tree with his wingtip and plunged into a ditch. The aircraft exploded and burst into flames, killing William and his co-pilot, Vyrell Mitchell.

The death of the ageing David, not all that long before, had not been unexpected. William's death, at such a young age, was a shattering blow to the family and

183

Elizabeth, at Balmoral when the news reached her, immediately cancelled her planned visit to the Olympic Games in Munich. William's death meant an end too to Richard's hoped-for way of life as an ordinary working architect. Like it or not, he was now very much Prince Richard, heir to the earldom of Gloucester and shortly afterwards he and his young bride were to move from their terraced home in Camden Town to the more regal precincts of Kensington Palace.

Philip, when the news reached him, was already in Munich in his capacity as president of the International Equestrian Federation. Anne joined him there in time to watch Britain's eventing team in action, driving from jump to jump in a Land Rover. Whether or not her father noticed, she had eyes mainly for Mark. She was upset by his near-disastrous showing cross-country and equally wild with excitement when he had a clear round in the show jumping to assure Britain's victory. Richard Meade, the British captain, who jumped last, could have hit five fences and Britain would still have won. As it was, he hit none and took the individual gold medal to go with Britain's team medal.

That night the British team celebrated their victory with a visit to a local night club. Anne went with them. Gossip columnists reported next day that she had spent most of the evening dancing with Richard Meade. Their information was wildly inaccurate. It was she and Mark who were inseparable in victory.

The gossip columns were to get it right, however, in the weeks that followed. With Anne and Mark making a beeline towards each other each time they met, and once even appearing together in matching sweaters, it could hardly have been otherwise. Head over heels in love, Anne paraded her feelings for all to see.

But some things remained secret from the gossip columnists. There were romantic weekends together at Catterick, where Mark was then stationed, which no one except

Anne's parents knew anything about. Even Anne's maid was left guessing as to where she went from Friday evening to Monday morning. At Catterick, Anne made no attempt to disguise herself in a headscarf and dark glasses as Aunt Margo had done while being wooed by Tony. She went riding quite openly with Mark, out to dinner with him and even popped into a local pub with him sometimes for a quick drink. Somewhat surprisingly, few people seem to have recognised her on such occasions. She was, of course, easily enough recognised when she and Mark attended the regimental ball and again at the Bedale Hunt ball which they went to at Bolton Hall. And not only easily recognised at the hunt ball, but suddenly the focus of all eyes and the cause of whispers because of the loving way they were dancing together. Too late, they realised the stir they were causing and fled the ballroom in embarrassed confusion.

Anne's parents celebrated their silver wedding that November. Twenty-five years of marriage had flown in no time, it seemed. If their relationship had had its ups and downs in the beginning, it had long since settled on a more placid and companionable plane. The children were growing up. Anne was twenty-two that August and Charles celebrated his twenty-fourth birthday a few days before his parents' silver wedding. He was now a sub-lieutenant in the Navy, waiting to join the frigate *Minerva*, flitting happily from girl to girl during spells ashore. While not about to short-list eligible European princesses for him, as Gan Gan had once done for Uncle David, his mother was beginning to wonder when he would decide to marry, settle down and produce an heir to succeed both of them.

On a public level, Elizabeth and Philip marked their silver wedding with a thanksgiving service at the Abbey where they had been married and a celebration lunch at the Guildhall. But a wife's personal feelings showed in the speech the Queen made at the luncheon. Today of all days, she joked, she could surely be forgiven for starting her speech with the time-honoured royal cliché, 'My husband and I'. Clearly speaking from the heart, she went on: 'A marriage begins by joining man and wife together. But this relationship, however deep, needs to develop and mature with the passing years. For that it must be held firm in the web of family relationships, between parents and children, grandparents and grandchildren, cousins, aunts and uncles.' For her, it was a very rare public display of her personal emotions, with many of her own 'family web' present to witness it.

On a more personal level, the silver wedding was also celebrated with a palace party which Charles and Anne gave for their parents. Mark was one of Anne's guests. She knew now, for certain, that he was the man for her and it was high time for her parents to get to know him. She had already met his parents, and his sister, visiting them at their country home, making friends with the family dogs, Moriarty, Beckie and Janie, hiding in a horse-box for the short drive to his aunt's stables. She was at the stables so often, in fact, that village folk who caught a glimpse of her took her to be a new girl groom.

That Christmas, after spending Christmas Day with her own family at Windsor, she drove to Great Somerford to spend Boxing Day with Mark and his parents. She saw the New Year in with her parents at Sandringham, where Mark joined her a day later. They had a pleasantly romantic weekend, riding together each day, spending their evenings with heads close together as they tackled one of the giant jigsaw puzzles always to hand at Sandringham. When Anne went to church with her parents on Sunday morning, Mark did not accompany them. But he was there just the same, slipping in by a side door to join them in the family pew and disappearing the same way when the service was over.

It was his first period of sustained close contact with his future in-laws and, understandably, he was as unnerved and in awe as Philip had once been with Bertie. For their part, Elizabeth and Philip did their best to put him at his ease, calling him 'Mark' and treating him almost as one of the family.

He was again at Sandringham the following weekend, this time with news that his regiment was being posted to Germany. With a spell of separation ahead, he and Anne decided to cut church that Sunday. Instead, they saddled a couple of horses and went for a long, sentimental ride through the woods and fields. Later that day Anne drove him to Harwich to board the boat for Germany. She drove to the Navy Yard wharf and they sat in the car to say their goodbyes. But lovers find parting hard and Mark, after climbing out of the car, bent down and, oblivious of watching dock workers, kissed her again through the open window. Anne watched him board the *Prince Hamlet*, then drove back to Sandringham where she again saddled a horse, Mark's six-year-old Persian Holiday, and went for a solitary canter.

She told her parents that she wanted to marry Mark and they raised no objections. On the contrary, they liked him very much, they said, and were 'very happy' about the whole business.

Mark seized every opportunity to return to Britain from Germany. He and Anne went hunting together, shared an enjoyable reunion with others of the 1972 Olympic equestrian team and began schooling their horses in readiness for Badminton. He took her to have lunch with his parents and she had him home to Windsor for dinner with hers. By this time the newspapers were hot on the scent of another royal romance and the next time they went to school their horses at Alison Oliver's stables in Berkshire they found photographers lying in wait. Mark greeted them with a grin and a casual 'Hello, chaps', but the more temperamental Anne was somewhat put out. 'You're trespassing,' she snapped.

They continued to meet whenever Mark could slip over

from Germany. Photographers and reporters continued to haunt them. They continued to deny all suggestion of romance. 'There is no romance,' said Anne. 'We are just good friends,' added Mark.

Distracted as they were by all this, by love and the necessity for continuing to deny their love, neither of them shone at Badminton that year. Anne came eighth and Mark, with a disastrous round which saw him catapulted into the lake, came nowhere. But love scored its own victory. Mark proposed and Anne accepted.

Ahead, for Mark, lay the biggest ordeal of all. Anne may have accepted him, but it was still necessary for him to ask her parents for her hand in marriage. The problem was: Which parent should he ask? It was normally the father, but in this case mother was the Queen. Anne put him straight. Her marriage was a personal family matter, so Papa was the one to ask. Mark felt 'petrified' when he was shown into Philip's sitting room overlooking the rose garden at Windsor. However, popping the question proved to be less of an ordeal than he had envisaged. Philip could not have been more delighted, he said.

They were married in Westminster Abbey in November 1973. Coincidentally, the wedding day was also Charles's twenty-fifth birthday. Charles himself still seemed in no hurry to marry and perpetuate the family line. Like Uncle David before him, he seemed quite content for others – in this case, Anne and Mark – to do that while he remained footloose and fancy free. There had been quite a succession of girl friends over the years since Trinity, with Jane Wellesley, daughter of the Duke of Wellington, the latest favourite. They went on holiday together that year to her family's estate in romantic Grenada. 'No romance,' Charles insisted. The two of them were simply 'very good chums'. Unlike Anne and Mark, events were to prove that he was telling the truth.

Anne's wedding, for all that her parents insisted that it was a private family occasion, turned out to be a very public affair, a combination of state ceremonial and television spectacular, with twenty-five foreign Royals among the 1,600 invited guests. In the family circle there were the inevitable jokes. The favourite was that the couple's first offspring would probably have hooves instead of toes. The Queen loaned her daughter and son-in-law her royal yacht for a honeymoon cruise. Like Margaret and Tony before them, they had to make do with two single beds lashed together in place of the more usual first-night double bed.

It was just over thirteen years since Margaret and Tony had embarked on a similar honeymoon cruise. How idyllic everything had seemed at that time. 'We would gladly have lived in a little grass hut,' Margaret said on their return. How quickly their marriage had gone sour. With husband and wife both self-willed, there had been arguments almost from the start. Earlier they had ended in laughter and love. Unfortunately, more and more acrimony had crept in until private disagreements began to spill over in public. There had been a scene at an art gallery over so trifling a matter as to whether or not to buy a particular painting; another public squabble during an after-the-show party at Covent Garden. In recent years, they had increasingly spent more time apart. If this was partly from necessity, with Tony going overseas on photographic and film assignments, it was also partly from a realisation of the fact that they were happier apart than together. Margaret had taken to going on holiday alone to the villa they had built on the wedding gift plot of land on Mustique, while Tony retreated, also alone, to their cottage in Sussex. As they drifted apart, there was growing gossip of extra-marital romance. Much of all this, accurate in essence if less accurate in actual detail, found its way into the newspapers. Reading it, both Margaret's mother and elder sister were worried as to where it was all leading. Both hesitated to intervene in so personal and delicate an issue.

16

Divorce In The Family

Sandringham, like Balmoral, has long served as a form of
escape hatch for the Queen's family, a place to which they
can retreat at intervals and unwind from the pressures of a
life in which there is less and less personal privacy. Even
Sandringham, for the third and fourth generation of
Grandpapa England's family, proved to be far less of a
sanctuary than it had once been. Time was when the
family could move about there freely and casually. A few
hundred ardent loyalists might turn up on Sundays to see
them go to church, but for the most part they were
untroubled by public and press alike. Charles' love-life
throughout his twenties and into his thirties was to
change all that.

Whenever Charles was at Sandringham with others of
the family, the place would be besieged by photographers
and reporters, invaded by the curious in their thousands,
all hoping that he would have the girl of the moment with
him and that they would catch a glimpse of her. Charles
himself estimated that as many as ten thousand people
packed Sandringham Park and its approach roads the
Sunday morning he and Jane Wellesley went to church
there, not long after their romantic holiday in Grenada. It
was much the same with each fresh girl, busty blonde or
leggy brunette, who succeeded Jane in princely affection.
The possibility that this was it, the real thing at last, love

and marriage, the future Princess of Wales, the future Queen, was like an emotional magnet, attracting thousands to Sandringham, jostling and neck-stretching to view the latest light-of-love before or after church on Sunday morning.

No one, of course, paid any attention to the gawky teenager who sometimes, on holiday from school, trotted into the same church with her father and sisters a few minutes ahead of the Royals. Diana Spencer was thirteen the year that crowd of ten thousand people flocked to Sandringham to glimpse Jane Wellesley. Her father was not yet Earl Spencer and the family was still living at Park House on the Sandringham estate, which made her roughly equivalent to the girl next door, more an occasional companion to Andrew and Edward than to Charles. If she glimpsed and noticed him from time to time, he took no notice of her. Between them, in the early years of the 1970s, there was an unbridgeable age-gap. He was a man already while she was still a child.

The wonder is, as girl succeeded girl in his affections, that he survived bachelorhood long enough for her to grow up and catch his eye. If some of the girls with whom he dallied were no more than passing playmates and other relationships were blown up out of all proportion by the gossip columns, there were still one or two with whom he fancied himself to be seriously in love, one or two he came close to marrying. He was, at that time of life, a rather romantic young man who tended to fall in love all too easily. His mother was keen for him to marry and have children, and not simply to perpetuate the royal line. In her middle years, she was eager to have grandchildren around her, but with Charles unmarried and Anne seemingly more enthusiastic about horses than babies, saw little chance of that 'while I'm young enough to enjoy being a grandmother'.

Anne and Mark had moved into a five-bedroomed Georgian house at the Royal Military College, Sandhurst, where Mark was now an instructor. Their shared passion for horses showed in the decor. Everywhere there were pictures of horses, books on horses – they had been given no fewer than eighteen copies of the *Encyclopedia of the Horse* as wedding gifts – horse ornaments, horses on glassware and even on table mats. To keep in trim for competitive riding, both dieted regularly, favouring lean meat and green vegetables, foregoing such fattening items as bread and potatoes, butter and sugar. Anne, in particular, was in no hurry to have a baby. Pregnancy would interfere with riding. Certainly she did not see herself as bound to perpetuate the royal line. 'It's not a duty because I'm not a boy,' she argued.

Their friends were mainly of the horsey kind, met at equestrian events. As far as army life was concerned, they rarely socialised. A 'behaviour directive' sent out to other army wives at Sandhurst made it clear that there must be no social approach until they had first been formally presented, they must address Anne as 'Ma'am' and would have to submit their guest list for approval if they subsequently invited her round for coffee or dinner.

Just as his father-in-law had earlier been obliged to sacrifice his naval career, so Mark, shortly, was to be forced to abandon his army career. It was bound to happen. There were public duties Anne was obliged to carry out to justify her official allowance, so many times larger than her husband's army pay packet, and she wanted Mark with her. In those early days of marriage, they went together to South America, Australia, New Zealand and Canada. There was a spatter of public functions at home too. They were on their way back from a charity film show one evening, intending to stop at Clarence House to see Granny before returning home, when Anne found herself caught up in the most dramatic situation of her young life.

Their chauffeur slowed preparatory to making the turn into Clarence House. As he did so, another car cut in front of them and braked sharply. Anne and Mark, seated in the back with Anne's lady-in-waiting, Rowena Brassey, felt the jolt as they bumped into it. Almost before they realised what was happening, a man had jumped out of the car ahead and, gun in hand, was racing back towards them.

Anne's bodyguard, Inspector James Beaton, jumped down to intercept him. A bullet took him in the shoulder. He drew his own gun with the intention of firing back, but it jammed. Anne's chauffeur, Alex Callender, made a grab at the hold-up man and was shot in the chest. Across the road, a policeman Michael Hills, realised that something was wrong and sprinted towards them. He took a bullet in the stomach.

'Drop your gun or I'll shoot the Princess', the gunman threatened Beaton. Beaton had no option but to obey.

The man grabbed the rear door of Anne's car and tried to jerk it open. Mark, inside the car, tried desperately to keep the door shut. Wounded though he was, Beaton ran round the far side of the car, scrambled in and tried to shield Anne with his body. Another bullet took him in the hand.

As the wounded policeman leaned against a tree summoning help with his walkie-talkie, a passing journalist, Brian McConnell, stopped his taxi and tried to intervene. He was shot in the chest.

The gunman managed to wrench the car door open. He seized Anne by the wrist. 'Come on, Anne,' he shouted. 'I only want you for two days. I'll get a couple of million for you.'

As he tried to pull her from the car, Mark locked an arm round her waist to hold her back. It all happened so fast that she had no time to be frightened, Anne said afterwards. 'Don't be silly,' she told the gunman. 'Please go away and leave me alone.'

Ron Russell, a burly Cockney, had also spotted what was happening, stopped his car and raced to the rescue.

Anne jerked her hand free of the gunman's grasp and Russell lifted her out of the car through the far door. The gunman ran round the car to get at her and she scrambled back inside. Ron Russell confronted the frustrated gunman. He had discarded one gun and now had another. A shot whizzed past Russell's head and shattered the window of a cab which had pulled up behind. Russell moved in and hit him on the side of the jaw. More police were now running towards the scene. As the gunman went down, one of them, Peter Edmonds, threw himself on him and pinned him to the ground.

It was a badly shaken Anne who returned to the palace when it was all over. Her parents were away on a royal tour of Indonesia. She telephoned them to tell them what had happened. In Jakarta, it was early in the morning when the telephone rang. Her mother was still asleep and it was her father who took the call. Only when he was assured that Anne was all right did he wake his wife and tell her what had happened.

After talking to her father in Jakarta, Anne put in a telephone call to her brother, Charles. He was in the Navy now, watch-keeping officer aboard HMS *Jupiter* and Anne's call reached him at the US naval base at San Diego where the ship had called prior to taking part in manoeuvres in the Pacific.

The Queen, when she returned to Britain, was quick to show her gratitude to those who had helped her daughter. She gave Inspector Beaton the George Cross, the civilian equivalent of the Victoria Cross, which her father had devised and designed back in World War II. Ron Russell and Michael Hills were each awarded the George Medal. For Alex Callender, Brian McConnell and Peter Edmonds there were lesser awards. The gunman, a young schizoid named Ian Bell, was sentenced to be detained indefinitely in a secure mental hospital.

Charles in the Navy, Anne married, Andrew now following in Papa's footsteps at Gordonstoun and Edward, the youngest of the children, already at preparatory school . . . the fourth generation of the family was growing up fast. And at Barnwell Manor, Harry, the sole surviving child of Grandpapa England, was close to death. Sadly, he did not live to see his first grandchild. His daughter-in-law Birgitte had already had one miscarriage. With a similar miscarriage threatening her next pregnancy, she was rushed to hospital where a baby boy was safely delivered two months ahead of time by Caesarian section. But by then Harry had been dead some four months and Richard had succeeded him as Duke of Gloucester, so that the four pound two ounce baby born so dramatically was automatically Earl of Ulster. His parents christened him Alexander.

Among older members of the family it was a time for stocktaking. David, Mary, Bertie, George and Marina, Harry, were all dead. Harry's widow, Aunt Alice, lived on. So did Wallis, a sick woman in Paris. As she notched up three-quarters of a century, Bertie's widow, the Queen Mother, born the same year as the dead Harry, seemed as indefatigable as ever. Uncle Dickie, another baby of the year 1900, likewise seemed indestructible, as upright and craggy as ever, more and more a substitute grandfather to Charles, as he had been a substitute father to Philip. With Charles obliged to interrupt his naval career to journey to Nepal for the coronation of King Birendra, his great-uncle went with him. During a stopover in New Delhi Uncle Dickie showed him round the palace from which, as the last Viceroy, he had presided over the dying days of the British Raj. For Mountbatten, it was a nostalgically sentimental journey and never more so than the day he watched his great-nephew, the Prince of Wales, play polo on that same Jaipur ground that another Prince of Wales, David, his cousin and close friend, had played on in the far-off 1920s.

For Margaret and Tony, the year Charles visited Nepal, there were again rumours of divorce; again denied as they had been twice before. But this time the rumours were less wide of the mark. Margaret's marriage was going from bad to worse and she was joined at *Les Jolies Eaux*, her holiday home on Mustique that year by a companion named Roddy Llewellyn, a young man not much older than her nephew Charles.

Behind the scenes, in the privacy of the family circle, matters moved rapidly towards a climax. Tony was pressing for divorce and a few months later came the news that he and Margaret were splitting up. The two children, they agreed, should stay with their mother, with Tony having reasonable access. Tony had already moved out of their Kensington Palace home and Margaret arranged to settle some money on him so that he could buy himself a house elsewhere in London.

Margaret's mother and elder sister were both distressed that a marriage which had started out so full of high hopes and promise should have ended so disastrously and in such a comparatively short time. The Queen made no attempt to apportion blame. As devoted as ever to her unhappy younger sister, fond of her brother-in-law, she saw finally what some others had realised all along, that they were too alike to be compatible, both high-strung and temperamental, wanting their own way too much. In public she displayed her loyalty to and affection for Margaret by inviting her to the annual Trooping the Colour ceremony, to garden parties at the palace and having her with her in the royal box at Ascot races. If she could not show her regard for Tony in public to the same extent, she did so within the privacy of the family circle, inviting him as well as Margaret to the party with which she celebrated her fiftieth birthday.

Estranged though they were, Margaret and Tony were also together, their daughter Sarah sitting between them, when their son David was confirmed in St George's Chapel, Windsor. Elizabeth's son, Andrew, was confirmed at the same time and there was a family luncheon

196

afterwards at the castle. Margaret and Tony sat almost facing each other over lunch, but there was no recrimination, no bitterness. Almost as though separation had come finally as a relief to both of them, they chatted easily and freely with others of the family and even, briefly, with each other.

For cousin Alex and her husband, Angus, there were problems too around this time, though of a very different nature. Nothing was wrong with their marriage. What troubled them were business worries. At the time he married Alex, Angus was a director of Lonrho, a company which prime minister Edward Heath was to label 'the unacceptable face of capitalism'. Even before Heath made his criticism, Angus had been cautioned that his connection with Lonrho and Lonrho's involvement in Rhodesia carried a risk of 'scandal rubbing off on the Crown'. As a result, he subsequently resigned his post of executive director and two years later quit the board altogether. But now, in 1976, came a Board of Trade report into Lonrho's business activities which, in parts, was extremely critical of Angus. Angus thought the report's conclusions unjust and the criticism of himself unfair. He promptly resigned from all his other directorships. Alex did not feel that such drastic and sweeping action was really called for, but Angus was anxious not to embarrass his royal in-laws further. With 'no way that I can effectively clear my name', it was, he said, 'the only honourable thing to do'.

Andrew was sixteen that year he was confirmed at Windsor, already young man rather than a boy, almost as tall as his father and elder brother, towering over his mother and grandmother. He was much more competitive and self-confident than his elder brother had been at the same age. More Mountbatten than Windsor, and almost incredibly good-looking. When he went to Montreal with others of the family to watch the Olympic Games he was constantly besieged by adoring teenage girls, squealing at the sight of him, thrusting notes, photographs and telephone numbers to call into the hands of royal aides. 'Please give this to Andy.' Andrew revelled in it all. Charles, at the same age, would have shrivelled in horror.

The same sort of pop-star welcome awaited him when he returned to Canada the following year for a spell of Commonwealth schooling such as Charles had had in Australia. Teenage girls, braving the icy cold, shrieked with delight as he emerged from his aircraft on arrival while others, later, when Andrew turned out for the school's First XV at rugby, danced around in sweat-shirts bearing such slogans as ANDY FOR KING.

That was the year of his mother's silver jubilee. Was it really twenty-five years since her father had died and she had succeeded him as Queen? She had been a wife and mother even longer, of course, and her true happiness in her silver jubilee year came from the knowledge that she was to be a grandmother. When Anne told her that she intended to give up horse riding for a time and start a family, the Queen could not have been more delighted. She could hardly do enough for her daughter and son-in-law and what she did do was handsome in the extreme.

Mark was no longer as happy in the army as he had been earlier on. While he still liked actual army life well enough, he was concerned about future promotion. What he needed, he knew, was the wider experience which could come only from a spell of soldiering outside Britain. But because he was the Queen's son-in-law, many doors were automatically closed to him. The army was hardly going to send him to Northern Ireland where he would almost certainly become a special target for the IRA. West Germany too was riddled with terrorists at the time, who might try to mount an assassination or kidnap attempt. Then there was the problem of his wife, who did not want to be separated from him. Where he went, she would go, Anne said, and the extra security required to safeguard her outside Britain would be a considerable headache to the army authorities.

Unable to see a way out, Mark decided that there was no further future for him in an army career. But if he resigned, what else could he do? The generosity of his royal mother-in-law provided a way out. Digging deep into her private purse, the Queen bought her daughter and son-in-law a 730-acre estate in Gloucestershire complete with eighteenth century mansion, Gatcombe Park, plus an adjoining 500-acre farm. Mark resigned from the army and settled down to farming with Anne finally fulfilling that teenage dream of breeding and riding horses.

Anne herself, at the time her mother succeeded to the throne in 1952 and for some years after, had been second to Charles in the line of succession. Then, because sons take precedence over daughters however unjust that may seem in this era of sexual equality, the births of two more brothers, Andrew and Edward, had pushed her down a couple of rungs. Even so, she was still fourth in line at the time she had her baby. And the baby, because Anne's three brothers were all unmarried and childless, ranked fifth. For all that, he came into the world without any sort of royal title. His mother might be a princess, but royal status could not be handed down automatically in the female line. And unlike Aunt Margo's husband, who, as Earl of Snowdon, had been able to pass on subsidiary titles to their children, Anne's husband had no title and did not want one. So the Queen's first grandchild was no more than plain Master Peter Phillips.

As it happened, Peter was born only three days before his maternal grandmother's pearl wedding anniversary, which was also, by coincidence, the day on which her cousin Richard's wife, the young Danish-born Duchess of Gloucester, gave birth to her second child, a daughter, Davina. Another member of the extended family was less fortunate, however. Cousin Eddy's wife, Katharine, had suffered a miscarriage only a few weeks earlier and had lost the baby she was expecting. The loss left an emotional scar which was to take a long time to heal.

With their new home at Gatcombe Park not yet ready for them, Anne and Mark had moved back into the palace ahead of the baby's birth and returned there for a few days afterwards. But Peter was not born at the palace. Prior arrangements had been made for Anne to go into hospital and when her contractions started in the early hours of the morning, Mark dressed and drove her there, staying on with her to witness the birth of his son.

The Queen was preparing for a royal investiture when Anne telephoned from the hospital to tell her she was a grandmother. The delighted mother and daughter chatted on the telephone for so long that the Queen was ten minutes late for the investiture ceremony, a very rare thing with her. 'My daughter has just given birth to a son,' she said by way of apology and explanation. She looked radiantly happy.

She looked equally happy when she drove to the hospital that evening to visit Anne and take a first look at her grandson. She was clearly overjoyed with her new role of grandmother and lost no opportunity of letting the public see her with her grandson. She posed with him for pictures taken by her Snowdon brother-in-law, was filmed with him as part of her annual telecast the following Christmas and also appeared with him briefly in the *Royal Heritage* television series. In the series, Peter was seen playing in 'The Little Cottage' which had been his grandmother's play place when she was a child. Now she had to crouch to get through the diminutive doorway of the cottage. The small girl who had once gazed at Grandpapa England through binoculars was now a grandmother herself, young-looking for the most part but every inch the kindly granny when she donned the glasses she now had to resort to for reading.

Any faint hope the Queen may have nurtured that her sister Margaret and brother-in-law Tony might patch up their matrimonial differences was doomed to disappointment. Margaret continued to be seen with the youthful

Roddy Llewellyn and Tony's eyes were similarly focused elsewhere. Their two years of separation were finally to end in divorce, granted on the grounds that the marriage had irretrievably broken down. It must have seemed bitterly ironic to Margaret that she, who had once been barred from marrying Peter Townsend because he had divorced his wife, should now herself be a divorced woman.

Their divorce left Tony free to marry Lucy Lindsay-Hogg, also divorced, a television researcher he had come to know when she accompanied him to Australia while he was out there filming an episode for a BBC series entitled *The Explorers*. No problem for the Queen in Tony's wish to re-marry. He was not a blood member of the family descended from George II and so did not need her royal consent. The problem would come if and when Margaret might think of re-marrying.

No fear of that, the younger sister assured the elder.

Yet another relative sought permission to marry around this time: cousin Michael, youngest child of Uncle George who had died so tragically in a wartime air crash, and sought it in curious circumstances.

Until the question of marriage arose, Michael had contrived to live a largely private life beyond the glare of the royal spotlight. Occasional achievements and upsets, as when he crewed the winning craft in a power-boat race or was banned from driving for exceeding the speed limit by a rather wide margin, had brought him into the headlines from time to time. These had been passing things and for the most part he had lived the first thirty-six years of his life unremarkably and unremarked upon, joining the army like his brother before him and reaching the rank of major. Then all at once, because he wanted to marry the Baroness Marie-Christine von Reibnitz, he was big news.

Problems arose because the Baroness was a Catholic whose first marriage had been annulled. She was Mrs

Tom Troubridge, accompanying her husband on a visit to Barnwell Manor, the country home of Michael's relatives, the Gloucesters, when she and Michael first met. If the Royal Marriages Act of 1772 requires all descendants of George II to obtain the permission of the reigning Sovereign before they marry, the 1701 Act of Settlement equally lays down that no one in line of succession to throne can marry 'a papist'. So Michael renounced his right of succession – no great sacrifice; he ranked no higher than sixteenth – and his cousin gave him her royal permission to wed his Catholic bride.

No one in the family was prepared for the furore which followed. It all hinged on whatever children Michael might have in the future. Despite their father's renunciation, they would retain their right of succession, it was stated, because they would be brought up as Anglicans.

However much this might accord with the Act of Settlement in Britain, it did not go down at all well with the Catholic hierarchy in Rome. The bride-to-be, it was said there, had previously given an undertaking that she would do 'all in her power to baptise and bring up the children as Catholics'. Pope Pius VI promptly banned the marriage from being solemnised in a Catholic church.

To keep the whole affair as low-key as possible, the couple had already decided to marry outside Britain. The Schottenkirche in Vienna had been picked as a suitable venue. The Pope's ban meant a hurried re-shuffle of plans, with Michael and his bride obliged to settle for a civil ceremony in the Vienna town hall.

Several members of the family – Anne, Michael's brother Eddy and sister Alex, plus Uncle Dickie – flew to Austria to lend moral support. The Queen herself could hardly attend, but she granted the bride, for all that she was a Catholic whose previous marriage had been annulled, the style of Royal Highness, a status which had been denied the divorced Wallis all those years before.

While the Pope's ban prevented the wedding being

the religious ceremony originally intended, the bride was still anxious that her new marriage should have the blessing of the Catholic church. This she achieved by attending a private mass the following morning, after she and Michael had spent their wedding night apart. Whether or not it was due to the church's blessing, the marriage quickly proved fruitful and their first child, a son Frederick, was born the following April.

17

Marriage For Charles

Gradually, over the years, Dickie Mountbatten had come to be looked upon as a member of the family for all that he was not actually born into it. He was descended, of course, from Queen Victoria, as the Windsors are also, though for him the path of descent lay not through Grandpapa England, but through Grandpapa's cousin, Victoria of Hesse, who had married Mountbatten's father, Prince Louis of Battenberg. The Battenbergs had become Mountbattens, at Grandpapa England's behest, at the same time that he took the name of Windsor during World War I.

Mountbatten's absorption into the family started in the days when David, dead now, had been a bright-eyed and bushy-tailed Prince of Wales. In the years leading up to David's abdication they were the closest of friends. In the years following the abdication Dickie became Bertie's friend too, though a shade less close perhaps. Bertie's wife, now disliking David as much as she had once been fond of him, was wary of anyone who had been close to him and some of that wariness rubbed off on her husband. Nevertheless, he was sufficiently close to Dickie to have him with them on that romantically fateful day in 1939 when Lilibet fell in love with Philip. Dickie was Philip's uncle, mentor, almost a father to him, and did much to urge his suit when he was courting Lilibet. She too, over the years of marriage, was to come to think of him affectionately as 'Uncle Dickie' and it was perhaps to please him, as well as out of love for her husband, that she changed her children's names to Mountbatten-Windsor. He was certainly proudly delighted at the linking of his adopted name of Mountbatten with the equally adopted royal name of Windsor. In the years which followed Bertie's death, 'Uncle Dickie' more and more filled the role of *pater familias*. It was he as much as anyone who sketched out the ground-plan for princely training which saw Charles go, by turns, to Trinity College, Dartmouth and into the Navy. 'My honorary grandfather', Charles would call him, jokingly but affectionately. Less jokingly and even more affectionately, he also spoke of him as 'a very special great-uncle'. But that was later.

Just as the Queen spends a large part of the summer at her Scottish retreat, Balmoral, so it was Dickie Mountbatten's custom to spend a week or so each year in Ireland, at Classiebawn Castle on the coast of County Sligo. Like Broadlands in Hampshire, Classiebawn, more Victorian mansion than castle in actual fact, had come into Mountbatten possession through his dead wife, Edwina. It had been a holiday home for the family ever since she inherited it from her father and the summer of 1979 found Mountbatten, erect and spritely still at seventy-nine, there as usual with his daughters, Patricia and Pamela, their husbands and children along for company. It was a happy family gathering and never more so than on the morning of 27 August, Bank Holiday Monday, when Mountbatten drove over to nearby Mullaghmore harbour where his boat, *Shadow V*, a converted clinker-built fishing boat, was moored. His elder daughter, her husband John Brabourne, two of their children, the fourteen-year-old twins Nicholas and Timothy, and John Brabourne's widowed mother went with him. They were off fishing. His younger daughter, her husband David Hicks and the rest of the grandchildren stayed behind at Classiebawn.

Aboard *Shadow V*, Paul Maxwell, the youthful deck-hand, had everything ready for the party and Mountbatten himself took the helm to nose the boat out of the harbour and head towards a string of lobster pots laid and baited the previous day. He looked every inch the retired old seadog in his knitted jersey sporting the badge of his wartime command, the destroyer *Kelly*.

He came up alongside the first of the lobster pots and eased back the throttle. As he did so, five pounds of gelignite secreted on board by the IRA during the hours of darkness, were detonated by remote control. It was 11.45 a.m. precisely.

'I'd rather snuff out in a hurry,' Mountbatten had said once. He got his wish. As *Shadow V* disintegrated into matchwood, he died instantly. One of the twins, Nicholas, and young Paul Maxwell died with him. The rest of the party were all seriously injured, Brabourne's mother fatally.

Philip, in France for some driving championship, a sport he had taken up since arthritis of the wrist forced him to give up polo, was stunned when news of Uncle Dickie's death reached him; so hard hit initially that he seemed to age ten years almost overnight. Elizabeth too was 'deeply shocked', while Charles, in Iceland on a fishing holiday, broke down and cried. The great-uncle who had been almost a grandfather to him would not have wanted that.

'I want no tears shed at my funeral,' Dickie had once said. 'I hope it will be a happy occasion. I am only sorry I will not be there to see the fun.'

If he could not be there, at least it went off exactly as he had planned it years before, with pomp and pageantry . . . almost as though a king had died, with military detachments from the United States, France and India as well as British and Gurkhas from Nepal honouring the coffin of the man who had been wartime Supremo in South East Asia. By coincidence, the funeral took place exactly thirty-four years, to the day, from the liberation of Singapore by troops of that 14th Army which Mountbatten turned from a defeated and dispirited outfit into a fighting force which disproved the myth of Japanese invincibility.

With his death, his elder daughter became Countess Mountbatten of Burma, with her son, Norton Knatchbull, now Lord Romsey, to carry the name and title on in due course. Just as he had planned his own funeral, so Mountbatten had arranged that too. With no son to follow in his footsteps, he had had a special clause devised at the time he was given his earldom to enable it to pass down through his daughter.

She and her husband, badly injured in the explosion, were still too ill to attend the funeral, but watched it on television. The dead Nicholas' twin brother, Timothy, was also suffering too much from his injuries to be there. But the rest of the grandchildren were all present, along with Mountbatten's younger daughter and her husband. So were the members of his 'adopted' family of Royals . . . Elizabeth and Philip, the Queen Mother, Andrew and Edward as well as Charles, Anne and Mark, Margaret, the Gloucesters, the Kents and the Ogilvys. Even Tony came, though sitting a little apart from the rest now that he had re-married in the aftermath of his divorce from Margaret.

Charles delivered the Address, grief more than bitterness in his voice as he spoke of the 'sub-human extremists' who had killed his great-uncle. The two of them had been talking of another visit to India together. There was now no possibility of that. Charles would still go, but he would go alone.

Charles and Philip wore their naval uniforms for the funeral. So did another of Mountbatten's honorary 'grandsons', Charles' brother Andrew, newly enrolled at Dartmouth at the start of a naval career, the fourth generation of Mountbattens (if not in direct line) to carry on a sea-going tradition which had started more than a century before when his paternal great-grandfather, Prince Louis of Battenberg, was a lad in his teens.

Prince Louis spent his life in the Navy. So did his son, the murdered Dickie. With no son of his own, it was Philip, the nephew he looked upon almost as a son, who followed Dickie to sea. Philip's naval career was cut short when his father-in-law died and it was necessary for him to play Consort to his wife's Queen. Now it was Andrew's turn. Nineteen pushing twenty at the time of Uncle Dickie's violent death, he had developed into a strapping six-footer, thrusting and competitive, perhaps a shade arrogant at times (which is also in the Mountbatten tradition) and as handsome as they come. Wherever he went, girls almost threw themselves at him and doubtless still do.

Had Dickie Mountbatten survived one year more, he would have celebrated his eightieth birthday a few months before Elizabeth, the widowed Queen Mother, celebrated hers. And what a birthday celebration that turned out to be, extending over a period of weeks. Six weeks ahead of her actual birthday there was a singing outburst of 'Happy birthday' as she cut the cake at a garden party given in her honour by the National Trust. The following month, still well ahead of her actual birthday, there was another garden party for her, given by her elder daughter at Buckingham Palace, and a carriage drive to St Paul's cathedral for a service of thanksgiving.

Again, the family turned out in force, but this time in gratitude and celebration, not grief, elder daughter and son-in-law, younger daughter and her divorced husband (Tony again sitting slightly apart from the rest), her Windsor and Armstrong-Jones grandchildren, all those others to whom she was related through her marriage to the dead Bertie. Only her great-grandson Peter was missing. Not yet three, he was considered too young to sit through it all.

From St Paul's they all went back to the palace for a

family luncheon party. 'A marvellous day,' the Queen Mum summed it all up. At her Clarence House home, tables, desks, even the floor itself, were fast disappearing under the avalanche of cards, telegrams, bouquets and gifts streaming in. Well ahead of the birthday her staff already estimated the total of cards and telegrams at around ten thousand and there were yet more on the day itself, plus a barrage of flowers from the crowd which gathered outside the house to sing 'Happy Birthday' and 'For she's a jolly good fellow' alternately. Others of the family came for a birthday lunch and accompanied her in the evening to the Royal Opera House for a gala performance of the ballet *Rhapsody* which Sir Frederick Ashton had created in her honour. Elizabeth and Philip were there along with the children, Mark, Margaret, and Harry's widow, Alice, the only other survivor of the Queen Mum's generation of the family, with the exception of Wallis, slowly fading away in Paris. ·

Earlier that year Alice had become a grandmother for the third time when her Danish-born daughter-in-law produced a sister for Alexander and Davina. They named the new baby Rose with two of little Rose's cousins, Elizabeth's youngest son, Edward, and Margaret's daughter, Sarah, as youthful godparents.

The Queen Mother's protracted birthday celebrations over, the family headed north as usual for the customary long summer stay at Balmoral. Because the paperwork of monarchy follows wherever she goes, even at Balmoral, even on holiday, the Queen must always have at least some of her staff to hand and among those who accompanied her to Balmoral in the late summer of 1980 was her assistant private secretary, Robert Fellowes.

Robert Fellowes was perhaps more familiar with Sandringham than Balmoral. Son of the man who was the Royal Family's agent at Sandringham for many years, he grew up there. Growing up at the same time at nearby Park House were the three young daughters of Viscount

Althorp (who later became Earl Spencer), and like many another man Robert ended up marrying the girl next door, as it were – Jane, the middle sister.

Jane, who had not long since given birth to her first child, accompanied him to Balmoral and, needing help with the baby, was joined there in due course by her younger sister, Diana, who knew all about babies through her work as a children's nanny and kindergarten teacher. Charles arrived there around the same time to stay with his parents.

Diana was no stranger to him. If he had taken little notice of the leggy schoolgirl who was sometimes at Sandringham parish church on Sunday mornings with her parents when he was there with his, he had taken increasing notice of her in more recent times when they ran into each other at the various social functions to which they were separately invited. She was nineteen now, tall and attractive, fair-haired and blue-eyed, eminently noticeable, and meeting her again at Balmoral Charles found himself falling in love.

It was not the first time in his still young life that the Queen's eldest son had fancied himself in love. There had been girls in his life before, some passing fancies and some more serious attachments. On at least one occasion, he had come close to proposing marriage, but the girl concerned had shied away from the idea of marrying into the Royal Family and the life in a goldfish bowl which would inevitably ensue.

What would Diana's reaction be to the idea of marriage? Was he really in love with her? And did she feel the same way about him? These were the questions uppermost in his mind as the two of them walked and talked together during that summer stay at Balmoral. Clearly more time was needed to provide the answers.

It was Granny who came to the rescue, delighted to play a part in giving young love an opportunity to blossom. Charles was her favourite grandchild; Diana the daughter of her oldest and closest friend, Ruth Lady Fermoy. Nothing would please her more than for them to marry. So later that year, with the rest of the family back home in London, she invited Diana to spend a few days with her at Birkhall, her home on the Balmoral estate. With Granny as chaperone, Charles joined them at Balmoral.

The Queen was also delighted with the course of events. Like Queen Mary before her, she had been concerned for some time that her eldest son had not yet found himself a suitable bride. She had known Diana almost since she was born, her parents and grandparents before her, though she had never been as close to any of the family as her mother was to Diana's grandmother. She liked the girl, considering her eminently suitable as both a daughter-in-law and Princess of Wales, and she too did what she could to help things along. That November she invited Diana to Sandringham for a family party to celebrate Charles' thirty-second birthday and she was delighted, early the following year, when Charles broke the news that he had proposed marriage to Diana and been accepted. Anne too had exciting news to tell her mother around this time. At thirty she was again pregnant.

Anne, being Anne, took the matter of pregnancy, or pretended to take it, rather casually. Childbirth was 'an occupational hazard for a wife', she quipped. Being pregnant was 'rather boring', she sighed. She was not 'particularly maternal in outlook', she insisted. All the same, she was as thrilled as any other young mother that May when she gave birth to her second child, a daughter. Her cousin Michael's wife had similarly given birth to her second child, also a daughter, not long before. The Kents named their latest addition Gabriela, a perhaps rather exotic name which others of the family promptly shortened to 'Ella'. Anne and Mark gave their baby an equally unusual name, Zara.

All in all, 1981 was fast turning into a very happy year

for the Queen and her family if not for everyone else in a Britain plagued by inflation, unemployment, strikes and violence. Anne was now a mother twice over and Charles finally engaged to be married. Andrew celebrated his twenty-first birthday and Edward, the youngest and quietest of the Queen's brood, told his parents that he would very much like to follow in Charles' footsteps and go to university when his schooldays at Gordonstoun were over.

In the extended family circle too there was cause for delight. The widowed Aunt Alice was looking forward to celebrating her eightieth birthday at Christmas and in the June Eddy and Kate Kent quietly celebrated their china wedding anniversary, marking twenty years of marriage. But uppermost in everyone's minds, the cause of most excitement for weeks beforehand, was Charles' marriage to Diana.

They were married in St Paul's Cathedral on 29 July. With the exception of such newborn babes as Zara and Gabriela, almost the whole family rallied round to give bride and groom a right royal send-off . . . parents, Granny, uncles, aunts, cousins, in-laws, Gloucesters, Kents, Ogilvys, Philip's relatives from Germany, the daughters and grandchildren of the murdered Uncle Dickie. It seemed a pity that he himself could not have lived to be there. With his love of pageantry and splendour, he would have revelled in the ceremony of the occasion. Still the youngest of his granddaughters, India Hicks, was one of the five bridesmaids.

Margaret's daughter, Sarah, was chief bridesmaid, handling the bride's twenty-five feet of train with experienced aplomb. Eddy Kent's younger son, Nicholas, was one of the two pageboys. Charles had not one but two best men (or supporters, as the Royals have called them since Edward VII first started the fashion more than a century ago). They were, of course, his brothers, Andrew and Edward, the latter shooting up so fast at seventeen as to threaten to outstrip his father and brothers alike in ultimate loftiness. There was some slight concern in the family until a few days beforehand that the Queen Mum might not be able to make it to the wedding. A leg injury sustained when she slipped on some steps at Ascot had become infected. However, make it she did. 'I wouldn't have missed it for anything,' she told others of the family. In fact, she had had the bride and the bride's grandmother to stay with her overnight and it was from Clarence House that Diana was married.

The wedding was easily the most glittering and heart-warming family occasion since – indeed, more glittering than – the Queen's own wedding nearly thirty-four years earlier. Like most weddings, it also had its mishaps and its moments of informality. With bride and groom alike keyed up and nervous, both fluffed their lines somewhat, Diana marrying 'Philip Charles' instead of Charles Philip and Charles agreeing to share *her* worldly goods instead of undertaking to share his own. But it was through no slip of the tongue that the youthful Diana did not promise to obey her husband. If it was not the first time that particular promise had not been made at a Royal Family wedding – the Danish-born bride of Richard of Gloucester had similarly omitted it – it was the first time for a bride almost certainly destined to be the future Queen. Andrew, as much a joker at twenty-one as he had been in childhood, was mainly responsible for the informal touches which highlighted the occasion. He talked bride and groom into kissing each other on the palace balcony in full view of everyone. Grandpapa England, with his high sense of the fitness and propriety, would certainly not have approved. And it was Andrew too who unexpectedly produced the large 'Just Married' placard which adorned the carriage in which the newlyweds trotted off on honeymoon.

While there were some 2,500 guests at the wedding ceremony in St Paul's, the wedding breakfast was restricted to members of the family, their new Spencer in-laws and a few favoured friends. It would have been difficult to accommodate more, so large had the family itself grown over the years . . . far bigger in 1981 than when Grand-papa England first gave it the name of Windsor in 1916 . . . and getting larger and larger, through marriage and childbirth, with the years.

The Queen, on her own silver wedding anniversary nearly nine years before, was speaking from the heart when she referred to the family 'web' which binds parents and children, grandparents and grandchildren, uncles, aunts and cousins. She feels deeply that the real strength of a nation derives from the union of its individual families. She is proud of the fact that hers is a particularly 'united' family; that the 'web' which binds it has become stronger and more extended with each generation.

The births of a son and a daughter to Princess Anne had already made the Queen a grandmother, and now, with the marriage of Prince Charles, she could hopefully antici-pate not only more grandchildren, but that all-important firstborn child of a firstborn son who would provide a direct line of succession to the throne.

She did not have long to wait. It was only a few weeks after that July wedding at St Paul's that Diana, on holiday with her royal in-laws at Balmoral, confided that she was already pregnant.

Boy or girl, the expected baby would be next in line of succession after Papa (Prince Charles). But a firstborn girl would maintain that position only if Charles and Diana did not have a son later, however unfair that might seem in this age of sexual equality. So hopes were high for a boy.

And a boy it turned out to be, a sturdy blue-eyed babe of 7 pounds 1½ ounces who 'cried lustily', according to Charles, to announce his arrival into the family. The baby was born in a private room at St Mary's hospital, London, on 21 June 1982. Diana was not quite twenty-one at the

214

time and she and Charles had not yet been married a full eleven months.

A prince from birth, like his father before him, the new arrival was christened William Arthur Philip Louis in the presence of a family gathering which included not only the proud parents and the Queen and Philip as grandparents, but a great-granny in the person of the Queen Mother as well as two of the Queen's other three children, Anne and Edward, and her cousin, Princess Alexandra. Alexandra was one of the god-parents. Lord Romsey, grandson of Philip's murdered Uncle Dickie was another. Missing from the family gathering, however, was the Queen's other son, Prince Andrew. He was otherwise engaged at the time as a helicopter pilot aboard HMS *Invincible*, still busy in the South Atlantic following the recapture of the Falkland Islands.

Monarchy and family being so intricately intertwined, it was not only a new grandchild the Queen held in her arms the day of the christening, but the nation's future King . . . little Prince William of Wales. To his grandmother, of course, he is simply William, another, though rather special, grandchild, to be loved and enjoyed, watched and watched over, during the years of growing up.

The tall, narrow house in Piccadilly, where the Queen herself spent her early childhood and where she once stood at an upstairs window, peering through binoculars at her own beloved grandfather, no longer exists. It was demolished by German bombs during World War II. But grandparents being what they are, doubtless 'Grandmama England' will find some other vantage point from which this rather special grandchild, in the years ahead, can also play the I-spy game Grandpapa England once played with her.

Bibliography

We have found the following books especially instructive and recommend them to those who may wish to know more about the individual members of the Queen's family.

HRH Princess Marina, Duchess of Kent – J. Wentworth Day, Robert Hale, 1962.

The Princesses Royal – Geoffrey Wakeford, Robert Hale, 1973.

Prince Henry, Duke of Gloucester – Noble Frankland, Weidenfeld & Nicholson, 1980.

King George V – John Gore, John Murray, 1941.

Queen Mary – J. Pope Hennessy, Allen & Unwin, 1959.

Double Exposure – Gloria Vanderbilt & Thelma Lady Furness, Fredk. Muller, 1959.

Time & Chance – Peter Townsend, Collins, 1978.

Thirty Years A Queen – Geoffrey Wakeford, Robert Hale, 1968.

King George VI – J. Wheeler-Bennett, Macmillan, 1958.

Edward VII – Frances Donaldson, Weidenfeld & Nicholson, 1974.

The Heart Has Its Reasons – The Duchess of Windsor, Michael Joseph, 1956.

Queen of Tomorrow – Louis Wulf, Sampson Low, Marston & Co, 1946.

Mountbatten, Hero Of Our Time – Richard Hough, Weidenfeld & Nicholson, 1980.

STAR BESTSELLERS

0352 309350	**WHISPERS** Dean R Koontz (GF)	1.95*
0352 310804	**ROGUE OF GOR** John Norman (Sci. Fantasy)	2.25*
0352 310413	**AFTERMATH** Roger Williams (GF)	1.60
0352 310170	**A MAN WITH A MAID** Anonymous (GF)	1.60*
0352 310928	**A MAN WITH A MAID VOL. II** Anonymous (GF)	1.75
0352 395621	**THE STUD** Jackie Collins (GF)	1.75
0352 300701	**LOVEHEAD** Jackie Collins (GF)	1.50
0352 398663	**THE WORLD IS FULL OF DIVORCED WOMEN** Jackie Collins (GF)	1.75
0352 398752	**THE WORLD IS FULL OF MARRIED MEN** Jackie Collins (GF)	1.75
0352 311339	**THE GARMENT** Catherine Cookson (GF)	1.25
0426 163524	**HANNAH MASSEY** Catherine Cookson (GF)	1.35
0426 163605	**SLINKY JANE** Catherine Cookson (GF)	1.25
0352 310634	**THE OFFICERS' WIVES** Thomas Fleming (GF)	2.75*
0352 302720	**DELTA OF VENUS** Anais Nin (GF)	1.50*
0352 306157	**LITTLE BIRDS** Anais Nin (GF)	1.25*
0352 310359	**BITE OF THE APPLE** Molly Parkin (GF)	1.50

*Not for sale in Canada

Prices are subject to alteration

STAR BESTSELLERS

0352 311010	**CARDINAL SINS** Andrew M. Greeley (GF)	1.95*
0352 310723	**THE ANALOG BULLET** Martin Cruz Smith (GF)	1.50*
0352 310715	**THE INDIANS WON** Martin Cruz Smith (GF)	1.50*
0352 312513	**LOVING FEELINGS** Kelly Stearn (GF)	1.75
0352 312823	**FLIGHT 902 IS DOWN** H. Fisherman & B. Schiff (Thriller)	1.95*
0352 397403	**DOG SOLDIERS** Robert Stone (Thriller)	1.95*
0352 312408	**THE WARRIOR WITHIN** S. Green (Sci. Fic.)	1.75*
0352 312491	**FRIDAY 13TH III** Michael Avallone (Horror)	1.60*
0352 312017	**SLUGS** Shaun Hutson (Horror)	1.60
0352 306866	**DEATH TRIALS** Elwyn Jones (Gen. Non. Fic.)	1.25
0352 398108	**IT'S BEEN A LOT OF FUN** Brian Johnston (Bio)	1.80
0352 311487	**BING THE HOLLOW MAN** Shepherd & Slatzer	1.75*
0352 303506	**THE UNINVITED** Clive Harold (unexplained)	1.50
0352 310022	**BARRY MANILOW** Tony Jasper (Music)	1.50
0352 301961	**A TWIST OF LENNON** Cynthia Lennon (Music)	1.25

* Not for sale in Canada   Prices are subject to alteration

STAR BESTSELLERS

0352 300965	**LONELINESS OF THE LONG-DISTANCE RUNNER** Alan Sillitoe (GF)	1.60
0352 300981	**SATURDAY NIGHT AND SUNDAY MORNING** Alan Sillitoe (GF)	1.35
0352 310863	**BEST FRIENDS** Kelly Stearn (GF)	1.75
0352 310456	**GHOSTS OF AFRICA** William Stevenson (GF)	1.95*
0352 300078	**THE FIRST DEADLY SIN** Lawrence Sanders (Thriller)	1.95*
0352 30099X	**DIRTY HARRY** Philip Rock (Thriller)	1.25*
0352 307390	**THE GOOD THE BAD AND THE UGLY** Joe Millard (Western)	1.25
0352 305231	**CROSSFIRE TRAIL** Louis L'Amour (Western)	1.25*
0352 312858	**THE SUNSET WARRIOR** Eric Van Lustbader (Sci Fic.)	1.95*
0352 312874	**SHALLOWS OF NIGHT** Eric Van Lustbader (Sci Fic.)	1.95*
0352 312866	**DAI-SAN** Eric Van Lustbader (Sci. Fic.)	1.95*
0352 309237	**101 REASONS NOT TO HAVE SEX TONIGHT** I M Potent, M.D. (Humour)	1.25*
0352 396121	**BODYGUARD OF LIES** Anthony Cave Brown (Gen. Non. Fic.)	2.50*
0352 310731	**PERSONAL COMPUTERS** Peter Rodwell (Gen. Non. Fic.)	1.50

*Not for sale in Canada   Prices are subject to alteration

STAR Books are obtainable from many booksellers and newsagents. If you have any difficulty please send purchase price plus postage on the scale below to:-

Star Cash Sales
P.O. Box 11
Falmouth
Cornwall
OR
Star Book Service,
G.P.O. Box 29,
Douglas,
Isle of Man,
British Isles.

While every effort is made to keep prices low, it is sometimes necessary to increase prices at short notice. Star Books reserve the right to show new retail prices on covers which may differ from those advertised in the text or elsewhere.

Postage and Packing Rate

UK: 45p for the first book, 20p for the second book and 14p for each additional book ordered to a maximum charge of £1.63. BFPO and EIRE: 45p for the first book, 20p for the second book, 14p per copy for the next 7 books thereafter 8p per book. Overseas: 75p for the first book and 21p per copy for each additional book.